Reforming Collateral Laws to Expand Access to Finance

Heywood Fleisig
Mehnaz Safavian
Nuria de la Peña

THE WORLD BANK
Washington, D.C.

ISBN: 0-8213-6490-1
E-ISBN: 0-8213-6491-X
13-digit ISBN: 978-0-8213-6490-1
DOI: 10.1596/978-0-8213-6490-1

Library of Congress Cataloging-in-Publication data has been applied for.

CONTENTS

ACKNOWLEDGMENTS

The authors thank Irene Arias, Spiros Bazinas, Charles Cadwell, Ronald C. C. Cuming, Frédérique Dahan, Alejandro Alvarez de la Campa, Simeon Djankov, Aurora Ferrari, Mario Fischel, Matthew Gamser, Alejandro Garro, Lance Girton, Roy Goode, Steven Harris, Rochelle Hilton, Martin Holtman, Nick Klissas, Richard Kohn, Boris Kozolchyk, Anjali Kumar, Jinchang Lai, Peter Mousley, Vincent Palmade, and John Simpson for excellent and thoughtful comments. In addition, the authors gratefully acknowledge the assistance of a background document by Yair Baranes and Ronald C. C. Cuming, "A Manual for Creating & Implementing Modern Secured Financing Systems" (available from Mehnaz Safavian at the World Bank). They thank the World Bank Group's Small and Medium Enterprise Department and the government of the Netherlands for financial support. Finally, they thank Alison Strong for excellent editorial support. The helpful comments and assistance notwithstanding, the views expressed here are those of the authors and do not necessarily reflect those of the reviewers nor of other staff of the World Bank, its executive directors, or the countries they represent.

INTRODUCTION

Most readers, especially those with a car loan or home mortgage, are familiar with the concept of collateral—property that a borrower pledges and that the lender can lawfully take away if the borrower defaults on the loan. Collateralized, or secured, loans are the most common lending contract in the formal financial sector, in developing and industrial countries alike. This makes sense from a lender's perspective: loan contracts can be more easily enforced when secured by collateral.

Loans secured by collateral are part of a broader set of secured transactions—transactions in which the parties agree to secure an obligation with an enforceable security interest in property. Besides a lender, the party accepting the security of collateral could be a business selling goods on credit or any other party needing a guarantee—such as a government contracting agency seeking a performance bond from a road construction firm. All these transactions are governed by a legal system that can dictate many things: how a security interest is created, who may create it, who has priority in receiving the proceeds from sale of the collateral, how security interests are made public, what rights other parties have in the property offered as collateral, how the property is repossessed in the event of default, how it is sold, and how the proceeds are used to satisfy the claim of the party who has the security interest in the property.[1]

Why a book on reforming the legal systems governing collateral—the laws of secured transactions, the archives for filing security interests, and the systems for enforcement? Because in countries that have not reformed these legal systems, most of the assets that firms hold cannot be used to secure loan contracts. These assets become "dead capital."[2]

Contrary to common belief, it is not insufficient assets that prevent firms in low- and middle-income countries from accessing finance. Indeed, firms have a wide array of assets that could easily be used to secure loans—movable assets from goods and machinery to accounts receivable and warehouse receipts. Unreformed legal systems limit the use of such assets as collateral and therefore limit access to credit by leading to both higher interest rates and smaller loan volumes. That means lower investment and slower economic growth.

WHAT THE BOOK AIMS TO DO

This book on reforming the legal systems governing collateral is directed to task managers in multilateral institutions, policymakers in developing countries, and staff of international donor agencies who would like to learn more about the reform—why it is important, how to implement it and what challenges to expect in the process, what resources are needed, and what impact can be expected.

Reforming the legal framework for secured transactions requires a new law governing the use of movable property as collateral and a modern filing archive to make public the claims against such property. A continuing challenge for task managers and policymakers will be to understand, explain, and justify the reform. Why is collateral important, and how does it expand access to credit? Chapter 1 explains. It also provides evidence of the potential benefits of the reform and of the costs associated with maintaining the status quo, evidence that can be used in making the case for reform to stakeholders—both government officials and interest groups.

The reform not only has important direct effects; it also supports and reinforces other donor-supported reforms aimed at strengthening the financial sector. Chapter 2 explains how reforming the legal framework for secured transactions can bolster the financial sector effects of other reforms and even substitute for other, less successful interventions.

Achieving the desired economic effect from the reform will require some changes in the law governing secured transactions. Stakeholders often resist changes in law, hoping that changes in regulation, institutions, or training will do the job. They cannot, and task managers must be prepared to explain why. Chapter 3 shows how restrictions in the law can limit access to credit and how reforming the law would eliminate these restrictions. This chapter links reforms in the law directly to their practical effects—expanding the use of movable property as collateral, broadening the scope of secured transactions, promoting financial innovation, and improving the terms and conditions of credit contracts.[3]

Chapter 4 broadly discusses the content of the reform. The book does not provide a complete treatment of the law of secured transactions or a complete list of the features of such laws. Such treatments are available—often many times the length of this book (as are the laws themselves)—written by justifiably famous commercial lawyers (see the appendix for suggested readings). Designing a sound reform requires the assistance of a highly skilled lawyer with experience in drafting these laws. No book can substitute for that.

Once stakeholders have been convinced of the need for reform, the reform must be implemented. Chapter 5 provides practical guidance on how to do so. Some reform strategies seem to work well; others seem less effective.

Finally, the effect of the reform needs to be evaluated. Chapter 6 explains how to measure the economic gain from the reform.

HOW THE WORLD BANK HAS SUPPORTED REFORM

The World Bank's interest in secured transactions dates to the early 1990s, about the same time that the European Bank for Reconstruction and Development (EBRD) issued its draft model law for such transactions. Secured lending was one of several areas the World Bank explored in seeking to improve the flow of credit to firms with good growth prospects and to improve the condition of the poor by increasing their access to credit. The World Bank shifted its attention away from development finance institutions—which simply made loans that private lenders refused to make, with disastrous results. Instead, it focused on supporting reform of the underlying conditions in financial markets through its structural adjustment loans, its financial sector adjustment loans, and the Financial Sector Assessment Program jointly undertaken with the International Monetary Fund (IMF).

Attention to secured transactions grew in 1998, when the Group of 22 met and instructed the World Bank and the IMF to help reduce the incidence of financial crises by assisting in the reform of laws governing bankruptcy and secured transactions. Since then the World Bank has supported more detailed analytical work relating to the reform of secured transactions, particularly in its Doing Business initiative and Enterprise Surveys. This book is part of the continuing effort to support successful reform of this very important set of laws.

NOTES

1. The terminology surrounding collateral can be confusing, especially to those without a legal background. To be technically accurate, the book often refers to *security interests* and *secured transactions*. For the layperson, however, it is sufficient

to interpret these terms as broadly consistent with the notion of movable property serving as collateral for loan contracts.

2. A phrase applied to this problem by Hernando de Soto, most recently in *The Mystery of Capital: Why Capitalism Triumphs in the West and Fails Everywhere Else* (New York: Basic Books, 2000), chapter 1.

3. After this introduction, for reasons of space, time, and budget, the text confines its discussion of problems in the use of collateral to those involving movable property. Lending secured by immovable property, or real estate, though an important financial transaction, is extremely restricted in most developing countries. The high cost of using the mortgage excludes most smaller properties from serving as collateral. In addition, conventional mortgage laws can have little impact in countries where most property is not titled (most dramatically, transition economies and customary economies such as those in Africa and the Pacific). Other land rights—under leases, cooperative holdings, or customary ownership—though valuable, cannot serve as collateral because the legal framework does not support this. These are grave problems, but they are beyond the scope of this book. Broadly, these features underscore one general advantage of a system for lending secured by movable property: the underlying rights to such property are typically clearly defined, so a project to reform the laws governing its use as collateral can have a large and immediate impact.

CHAPTER 1

WHY COLLATERAL MATTERS

For those concerned with increasing the private sector's access to finance in low- and middle-income countries, collateral matters. It matters because of three essential features of formal credit markets:

- Borrowers face requirements for collateral in the formal financial sector of most countries, regardless of the size of the economy.
- Loans secured by collateral have more favorable terms than unsecured loans do, for any given borrower or size of loan. A borrower able to offer collateral can obtain a larger loan relative to the borrower's income, with a longer repayment period and a lower interest rate. This holds true regardless of the economy and of the other characteristics of the borrower. Conversely, a borrower who cannot provide the type of assets lenders require as collateral often gets worse loan terms than an otherwise similar borrower who can do so—or gets no loan at all.
- In most low- and middle-income countries most firms receive none of the benefits of collateral despite having a wide array of productive assets—because their assets cannot serve as collateral. This limitation arises entirely from the legal framework for secured transactions.

BORROWERS TYPICALLY FACE REQUIREMENTS FOR COLLATERAL

Secured loans are the most common loans in the formal financial sector. In low- and middle-income countries between 70 percent and 80 percent of firms applying for a loan are required to pledge some form of collateral (figure 1.1). In high-income countries the story is similar: in the United States, for example, 45 percent of all commercial and industrial loans from banks—and nearly 90 percent of those under $100,000—are secured by collateral.[1]

Why do lenders put such weight on collateral? The answer lies in the central question that private lenders confront: How can I ensure that I will be repaid? When lenders can obtain collateral from a borrower, it makes lending a less risky business. When they cannot, lenders must find other ways to reduce risk. That usually means less favorable terms for borrowers.

To reduce the risk of nonpayment, lenders try to gather a great deal of information about their borrowers. But information about borrowers tends

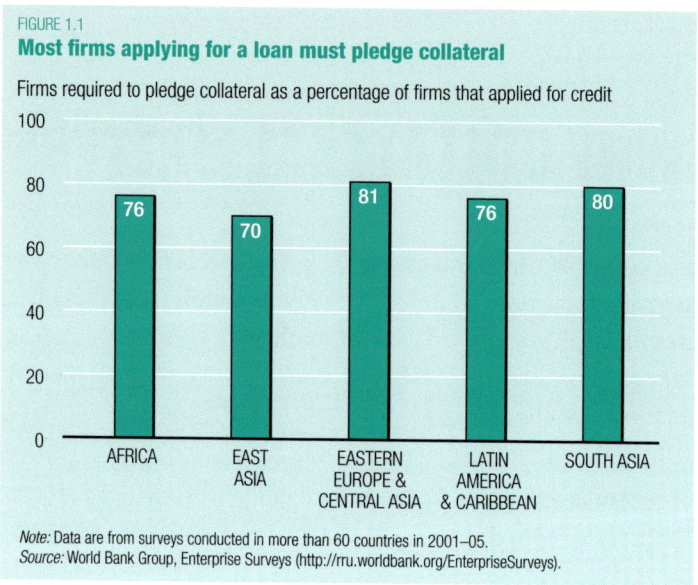

FIGURE 1.1

Most firms applying for a loan must pledge collateral

Firms required to pledge collateral as a percentage of firms that applied for credit

Note: Data are from surveys conducted in more than 60 countries in 2001–05.
Source: World Bank Group, Enterprise Surveys (http://rru.worldbank.org/EnterpriseSurveys).

to be difficult to get. In low- and middle-income countries credit reporting systems—if they exist—often contain only limited information, may rely only on data from banks, and may be available only to banks.[2] Moreover, typical borrowers lack audited financial statements; company records consist instead of checkbooks and canceled checks.[3] In many countries firms keep two sets of books—one for the tax collector and another for the accountant—a practice that undermines confidence in information from borrowers' balance sheets and income statements.

Ultimately only the borrowers know what they are going to do and what their true conditions are, while the lenders have to guess—a problem economists call asymmetric information. Lenders respond to this problem by doing business only with borrowers whom they have known and observed over many years.

Credit bureaus (where they exist) and records of prior performance can weed out those who failed to pay in the past. Identifying those who will not pay in the future is a bigger challenge. Careful analysis of borrowers, recognizing that those who will be in the market for a larger loan in the future are less likely to default on today's loan, helps spot good borrowing prospects.[4] But all lenders know that the facts in these analyses can change: good luck can turn bad; formerly conservative borrowers can be tempted by a high-risk, high-return project; healthy business operators or members of their family can get sick; and apparently honest business operators can turn out to be crooks. Even borrowers who have consistently repaid loans in the past may fail to repay a larger loan in the future. Lenders respond to this risk by increasing loan sizes very slowly.

Lenders also face uninsurable risks, risks that neither they nor the borrower can insure against: acts of war, natural disasters, even the death or illness of key employees of the borrower. The biggest causes of bankruptcy in the United States are death or illness of the borrower and natural or human-caused calamity. Lenders respond to this risk by diversifying their portfolios, limiting loans to any one borrower.

Together, these responses by lenders to the risks of lending create the credit market characteristics common in low- and middle-income countries:

- *Unsecured loans are small.* It takes a long time for lenders to learn about borrowers and for borrowers to establish reputations. So loan sizes start small and increase only slowly. The small loan sizes reflect not only credit rationing but also lenders' need to diversify portfolios to handle uninsurable risks.
- *Rates of interest are high.* Gathering information about borrowers is costly, limiting the entry of lenders; when lenders are few and have market power, they tend not to compete by lowering interest rates. The costs of information are even higher in isolated rural areas and where markets are segmented. In addition, interest rates must be high enough to compensate for the risk of default or for the high cost of monitoring that is sufficient to prevent default.
- *Repayment periods are short,* because all these risks grow with time.

Collateral can reduce the severity of these risks. Information on the good taken as collateral can substitute for information on the borrower, reducing the risks relating to asymmetric information. Collateral operates as broad insurance against uninsurable risk or intentional default leading to nonpayment of the loan, because sale of the good taken as collateral will provide funds for the lender. And as loan sizes grow, lenders can insist on more collateral.

Collateral also strengthens lenders' ability to collect. When a borrower defaults on a loan not secured by collateral, the unsecured lender must go through the judicial system to make a general claim on the debtor's property. The poor quality of judicial systems in many countries can make this a costly process with an uncertain outcome. Even if the judicial process works, the unsecured lender could still face many obstacles. The debtor might have no assets, because all assets might have been dissipated in the events leading to the default. Other lenders might have claims against the debtor's property. No matter the order in which loans were originally made, the lender with the fastest court procedure would get the assets needed to satisfy its loan before lenders working with slower courts. Or a bankruptcy court might divide the proceeds from the sale of the debtor's property evenly among the competing lenders.

By contrast, a secured lender can be confident that the collateral will cover the loan whatever the state of the debtor's other property. The secured lender would have a priority in the proceeds from the sale of that collateral, determined by the time it filed a public notice in the filing archive for security interests. Other lenders with lower priority, including unsecured lenders, would have no right to those proceeds until the secured lender's claim had been satisfied.

LOANS SECURED BY COLLATERAL HAVE BETTER TERMS

All these reasons not only explain why lenders require collateral. They also explain why lenders will lend considerably more to a borrower who can offer collateral than to one with the same cash flow or income who can offer only a signature—and why they will give that borrower more time to repay and a lower interest rate. The same is true for firms selling inventory and equipment on credit: these firms will offer better credit terms if they can take the goods they sell as collateral for the credit they give. Most readers know this from personal experience, having compared the terms of mortgages (loans secured by real estate, or immovable property) and car loans (loans secured by movable property) with the terms offered on credit cards (unsecured loans).

That loans secured by collateral, all other things equal, have more favorable terms than unsecured loans is easy to verify. Simply compare loan terms at any local bank branch, almost anywhere in the world. The terms offered by a credit union in the United States provide a good example (figure 1.2). A loan secured by movable property or real estate bears an interest rate about half as high as the rate on an unsecured loan. Moreover, for any given income of the borrower, a loan secured by real estate is about 10 times as large as an unsecured loan, and a loan secured by movable property about 4 times as large. Secured loans

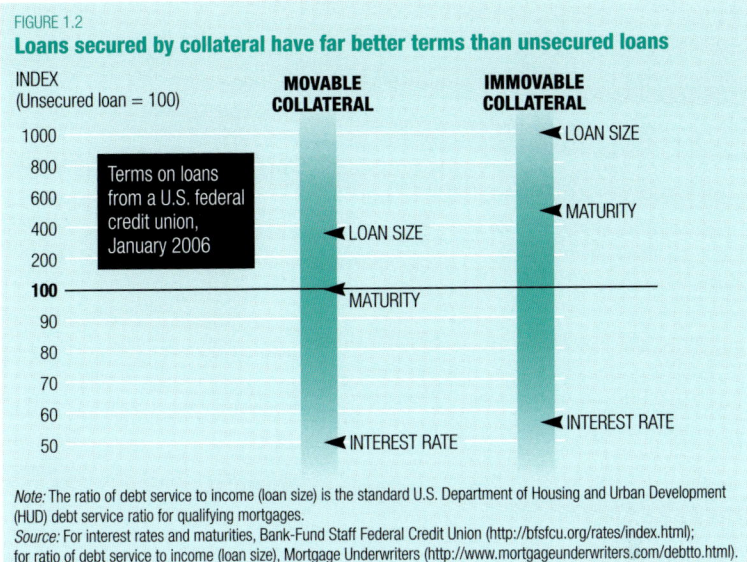

FIGURE 1.2

Loans secured by collateral have far better terms than unsecured loans

Note: The ratio of debt service to income (loan size) is the standard U.S. Department of Housing and Urban Development (HUD) debt service ratio for qualifying mortgages.
Source: For interest rates and maturities, Bank-Fund Staff Federal Credit Union (http://bfsfcu.org/rates/index.html); for ratio of debt service to income (loan size), Mortgage Underwriters (http://www.mortgageunderwriters.com/debtto.html).

also have longer repayment periods. The loan secured by real estate can be repaid over a period 5 times as long as that for an unsecured loan. This is the power of collateral.[5]

Collateral improves the terms of loans not only in countries with modern systems governing its use. Given a chance to work, collateral has the same effects in low- and middle-income countries. Take the example of Banco Solidario, a highly regarded microlender and commercial bank in Bolivia. A small borrower who can repay $87 a month, the amount needed to service the largest microcredit BancoSol offers, would get better terms if offering a car or real estate as collateral: an interest rate 20 percent lower, a loan 10–50 percent larger, and, with real estate, twice as long to repay (figure 1.3).

Collateral has an even greater effect on loan size for a higher-income client of BancoSol. A larger borrower who can pay the $820 a month necessary to service BancoSol's largest motor vehicle loan could get a loan 10 times as large as the unsecured microcredit by offering an automobile as collateral and a loan 15 times as large by offering real estate (figure 1.4). The effect of collateral on loan size increases with larger loans because BancoSol, like creditors everywhere, limits the absolute size of unsecured loans. Microcredit is often an effective vehicle for unsecured lending. But to get larger loans, for longer periods and at lower interest rates, borrowers at microcredit institutions must offer collateral.

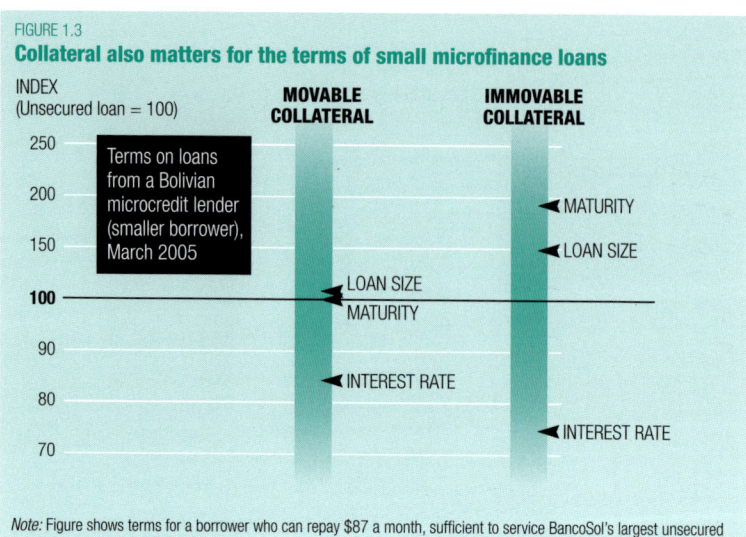

FIGURE 1.3

Collateral also matters for the terms of small microfinance loans

Note: Figure shows terms for a borrower who can repay $87 a month, sufficient to service BancoSol's largest unsecured loan. Interest rates derived algebraically from the terms of the loans shown on BancoSol's website.
Source: Banco Solidario (http://www.bancosol.com.bo/en/productors_cr.html).

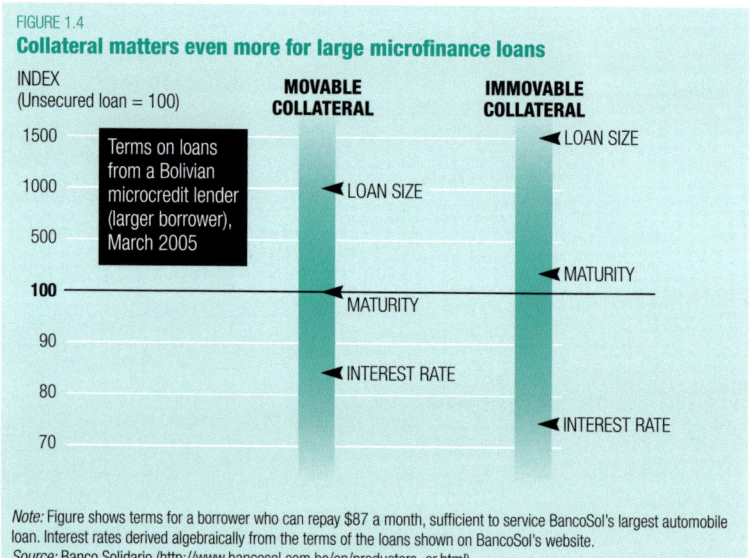

FIGURE 1.4

Collateral matters even more for large microfinance loans

Note: Figure shows terms for a borrower who can repay $87 a month, sufficient to service BancoSol's largest automobile loan. Interest rates derived algebraically from the terms of the loans shown on BancoSol's website.
Source: Banco Solidario (http://www.bancosol.com.bo/en/productors_cr.html).

MOST ENTERPRISES HAVE PRODUCTIVE ASSETS—
BUT CAN'T USE THEM AS COLLATERAL

Many policymakers believe that where firms in low- and middle-income countries cannot access finance, it is because they lack sufficient assets to serve as collateral. This is not strictly true: firms have assets that could easily be used

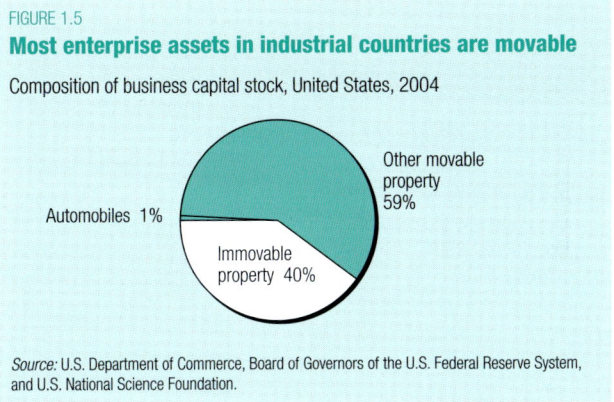

FIGURE 1.5

Most enterprise assets in industrial countries are movable

Composition of business capital stock, United States, 2004

Other movable
property
59%

Automobiles 1%

Immovable
property 40%

Source: U.S. Department of Commerce, Board of Governors of the U.S. Federal Reserve System, and U.S. National Science Foundation.

as security for loans—movable assets such as the goods they produce or process, the machinery they use in manufacturing, present and future accounts receivable from clients, intellectual property rights, and warehouse receipts. Around the world movable assets, rather than land or buildings, account for most of the capital stock of private firms and an especially large share for micro, small, and medium-size enterprises. In the United States, for example, movable property makes up about 60 percent of enterprises' capital stock (figure 1.5).

In the industrial countries with the most advanced legal systems for collateral—Canada, New Zealand, and the United States—lenders consider such assets to be excellent sources of collateral.[6] Most of the world's businesses face a very different situation, however. In most low- and middle-income countries only new motor vehicles or urban real estate can serve as collateral. For firms in some lines of business, such as urban transport companies, some heavy utilities, and commercial office buildings, this system of finance works. But for other enterprises it means that little of the property they own can serve as collateral.

A closer look at what makes up the movable capital stock tells more about the disparity in firms' ability to use as collateral the assets they have or will need to have as they develop. Firms in the United States hold movable capital stock in a wide range of categories, all of which would be considered excellent collateral by a U.S. lender (figure 1.6). Yet most of this capital could not serve as collateral in a low- or middle- income country with an unreformed collateral system. To take one example, nearly 99 percent of movable property that could serve as collateral for a loan in the United States would likely be unacceptable to a lender in Nigeria.[7]

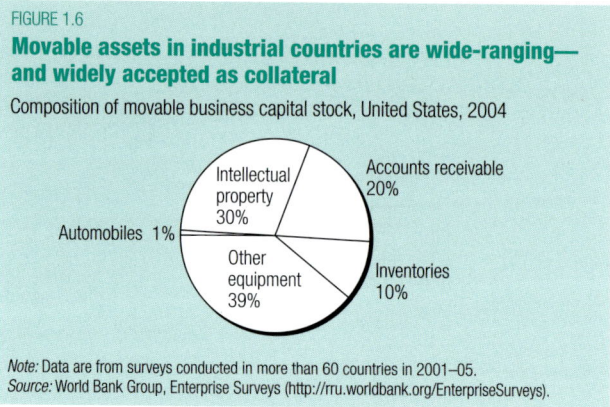

FIGURE 1.6

Movable assets in industrial countries are wide-ranging—and widely accepted as collateral

Composition of movable business capital stock, United States, 2004

Note: Data are from surveys conducted in more than 60 countries in 2001–05.
Source: World Bank Group, Enterprise Surveys (http://rru.worldbank.org/EnterpriseSurveys).

So there is a big mismatch in low- and middle-income countries between the assets firms have or will need to have and the assets lenders can accept as collateral (figure 1.7)—and it is this mismatch that is at the root of the lack of access to credit. Firms seeking to finance equipment that is not acceptable as collateral are often forced to rely on noncommercial funding sources, which can be both scarce and extremely expensive.

The problem does not lie in asset composition. The assets owned by enterprises in low- and middle-income countries reflect an optimal mix that is driven by technology, factor prices, and the needs of markets. Thus productive assets consist of a wide range of equipment, inventories, and accounts receivable—just as they do in industrial countries.

Nor is the problem that the benefits of using collateral are unknown in low- and middle-income countries. Indeed, where the collateral system works, these countries see much the same outcome as countries with modern systems do. To continue the earlier example, the interest rates for loans secured by automobiles in La Paz, Bolivia, differ from those in the United States by about the same amount as Bolivia's country risk premium.[8] Put another way, full macroeconomic stabilization in Bolivia would give Bolivians access to credit for purchasing automobiles similar to that enjoyed by U.S. residents.

The problem is that this effect of collateral does not extend to other movable property in Bolivia. So while U.S. borrowers can readily obtain loans for a broad range of movable property, Bolivian borrowers seeking loans for many of the same types of property could not even get interest rates quoted (figure 1.8).

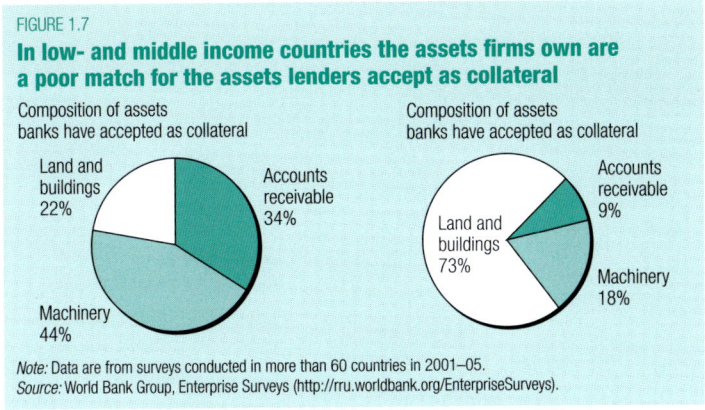

FIGURE 1.7

In low- and middle income countries the assets firms own are a poor match for the assets lenders accept as collateral

Composition of assets
banks have accepted as collateral

Land and buildings 22%
Accounts receivable 34%
Machinery 44%

Composition of assets
banks have accepted as collateral

Accounts receivable 9%
Land and buildings 73%
Machinery 18%

Note: Data are from surveys conducted in more than 60 countries in 2001–05.
Source: World Bank Group, Enterprise Surveys (http://rru.worldbank.org/EnterpriseSurveys).

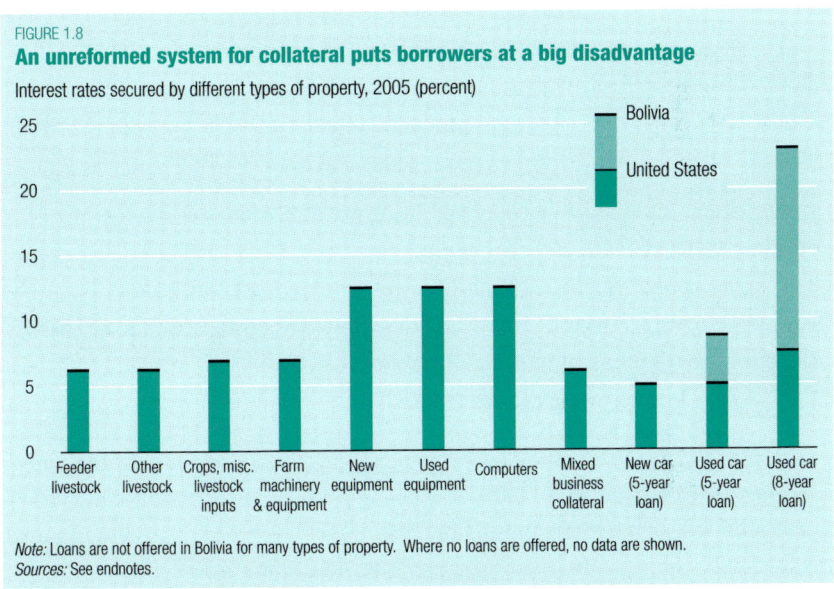

FIGURE 1.8

An unreformed system for collateral puts borrowers at a big disadvantage

Interest rates secured by different types of property, 2005 (percent)

— Bolivia
— United States

Feeder livestock · Other livestock · Crops, misc. livestock inputs · Farm machinery & equipment · New equipment · Used equipment · Computers · Mixed business collateral · New car (5-year loan) · Used car (5-year loan) · Used car (8-year loan)

Note: Loans are not offered in Bolivia for many types of property. Where no loans are offered, no data are shown.
Sources: See endnotes.

This example is not unique. In most low- and middle-income countries, once country risk premiums are removed, interest rates for loans secured by new cars or urban real estate are similar to those charged in industrial country markets.

What is the overall result of all this for businesses in low- and middle-income countries? Most firms face collateral requirements they cannot meet and get none of the benefits of collateral from the assets they own. For these

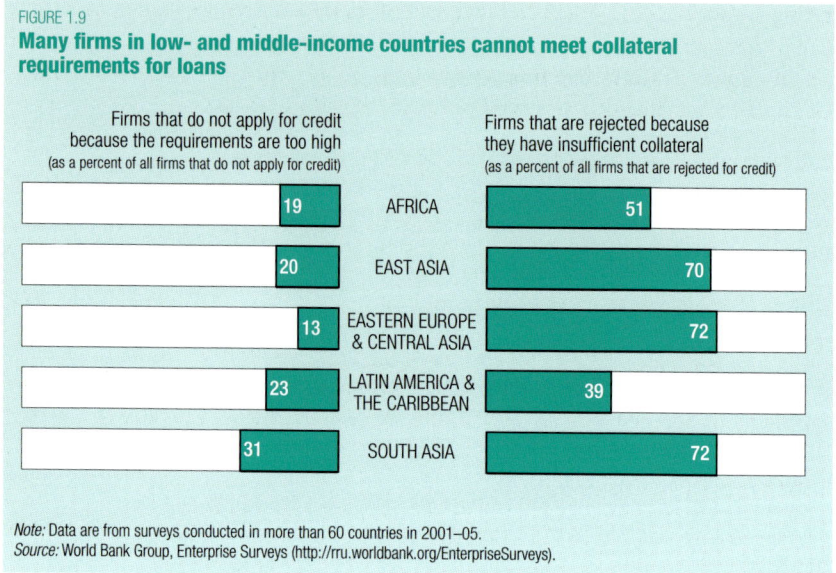

FIGURE 1.9

Many firms in low- and middle-income countries cannot meet collateral requirements for loans

Firms that do not apply for credit because the requirements are too high
(as a percent of all firms that do not apply for credit)

Firms that are rejected because they have insufficient collateral
(as a percent of all firms that are rejected for credit)

Region	Do not apply	Rejected
AFRICA	19	51
EAST ASIA	20	70
EASTERN EUROPE & CENTRAL ASIA	13	72
LATIN AMERICA & THE CARIBBEAN	23	39
SOUTH ASIA	31	72

Note: Data are from surveys conducted in more than 60 countries in 2001–05.
Source: World Bank Group, Enterprise Surveys (http://rru.worldbank.org/EnterpriseSurveys).

firms a lender's request for collateral does not represent an opportunity for better credit terms; it is code for refusal of a loan. Across developing regions, when firms apply for a loan or a line of credit, the most common reason that their application is rejected is insufficient collateral (figure 1.9). Entrepreneurs recognize this: firms around the globe report not bothering to apply for loans because they know in advance that they will be unable to meet the lender's requirements for collateral.

For these firms, then, reform of the laws governing the use of collateral is vital to unlock their "dead capital," increasing their access to the financing they need to raise their productivity and expand their operations.

NOTES

1. U.S. Federal Reserve System, Board of Governors, *Survey of Terms of Business Lending,* Federal Reserve Statistical Release E.2 (Washington, D.C., December 13, 2005; http://www.federalreserve.gov/releases/e2/current/default.htm).

2. The World Bank Group's Doing Business indicators rate credit information bureaus on a scale of 1–6, covering data reviewed, provision of historical data, data sources (including nonbank financial institutions), whether data cover both individuals and firms, and whether the data include positive as well as negative information. In 2004, of the 120 countries covered, only 14 received the highest

rating across all these categories (Stefano Stoppani, "The Importance of Private Credit Bureaus and the International Experience," presentation to Private Sector Development Regional Training Program, Istanbul, April 13, 2005; World Bank Group, Foreign Investment Advisory Service, Washington, D.C.).

3. For example, data from the World Bank Group's Enterprise Surveys show that, on average, only 53 percent of formal manufacturing firms have their financial statements audited. This share is likely to be much smaller in other sectors and among small, informal firms.

4. Jonathan Eaton, Mark Gersovitz, and Joseph E. Stiglitz, "The Pure Theory of Country Risk," *European Economic Review* 30 (1986): 481–513.

5. For more discussion, see Heywood Fleisig, "The Power of Collateral: How Problems in Secured Transactions Limit Private Credit for Movable Property," Viewpoint series, Note 43 (World Bank Group, Private Sector Development Vice Presidency, Washington, D.C., 1995).

6. The systems considered to be most advanced here are those allowing the largest share of movable property to serve effectively as collateral.

7. Authors' estimate, calculated on the basis of analysis from Ronald Cuming and Yair Baranes, "A Modern Secured Financing System Involving Personal Property Collateral for the Federal Republic of Nigeria" (report prepared for the World Bank, Africa Region, Private Sector Development Department, Washington, D.C., 2004), and authors' projections given movable property finance in the United States (for data sources, see figure 1.6).

8. Country risk premium is defined as the excess of the interest rate on local government dollar bonds over the interest rate on U.S. government dollar bonds of the same maturity.

CHAPTER 2

HOW COLLATERAL REFORM CAN SUPPORT OTHER IMPORTANT REFORMS AND INITIATIVES

Donors have supported many reforms to broaden and deepen the financial sector. Some of these aimed directly at increasing prudent financial intermediation. Some took an indirect path, relying on improved macroeconomic stability to correct financial imbalances or supporting judicial reform to improve contract enforcement and debt collection. Yet many failed to include secured lending initiatives.[1] As this chapter shows, reform of the legal framework for secured transactions, or collateral laws, supports and reinforces other important reforms targeting the financial sector. At the same time it expands access to credit in ways that these other reforms cannot duplicate.

BROADENING THE EFFECT OF MACROECONOMIC REFORM

Macroeconomic reform—aimed at reducing inflation and stabilizing exchange rates, for example—will improve access to credit. The reason is that extreme macroeconomic instability, accompanied by high rates of inflation and large, sporadic changes in the exchange rate, is almost always associated with higher nominal interest rates and shorter loan maturities, and often with higher real interest rates. Lenders always link the size of a loan to the borrower's capacity to service debt, and link that in turn to the borrower's cash flow or income. So, as a matter of arithmetic, higher interest rates and shorter maturities mean smaller loans relative to cash flow or income.

Macroeconomic reform, by reducing the country risk premium and the cost of the government's external finance, makes it possible to lower the interest rate on domestic debt and thus the rate that banks will demand on local currency loans.[2] The reform will therefore lower the general level of nominal and real interest rates and in this way improve access to credit. With a strong macroeconomic reform, interest rates on well-secured loans—loans with collateral that can be repossessed and sold in a way timely enough to cover a substantial fraction of the debt—can fall to levels similar to those in industrial countries. In most developing countries well-secured loans are those secured by new, registered motor vehicles—with new automobiles generally the most prized as collateral—and titled urban real estate.

Reforming the system of secured transactions can broaden this effect by extending the interest rate reductions to loans secured by movable property beyond automobiles, which amount to only about 1 percent of the movable capital stock (see figures 1.5 and 1.6 in chapter 1). With changes in the law that extend the benefits to the remaining 99 percent of movable capital—an amount nearly equal to GDP in most countries—macroeconomic stabilization will have a much broader effect on investment and economic activity. Without such changes, interest rates on loans secured by movable property other than automobiles will remain high because the rates reflect the large collection risk that only secured transactions reform can reduce.

Moreover, secured transactions reform can sometimes lead to interest rate reductions exceeding those from macroeconomic reform. The interest rate spread between loans secured by real estate and those secured by movable property other than automobiles can amount to 10–20 percentage points in countries with unreformed systems of secured transactions. In countries with modern (or reformed) systems that spread is only 2–3 percentage points. So secured transactions reform can reduce interest rates for loans secured by movable property other than automobiles by 8–17 percentage points. By contrast, macroeconomic stabilization could be expected to reduce the general level of interest rates by about 2–5 percentage points—the range for typical country risk premiums for developing countries and thus the amount by which their government borrowing rates would fall with stabilization.

The importance of the legal framework for secured transactions also shows up in private loans denominated in foreign currency. Exporters of internationally traded goods face little risk from domestic macroeconomic instability because the prices of their exports are fixed in foreign currency. For this reason a lender making a dollar loan to a producer of export commodities in a country whose currency is about to depreciate would actually face less risk than if the outlook for the exchange rate were stable. Depreciation would raise the foreign currency profit of the local exporter, making it easier to pay off the foreign loan. Yet lenders will not make such foreign currency loans—not because of macroeconomic risk but because they cannot reasonably expect to recover

BOX 2.1

Why Nicaraguan coffee is good collateral in New York but not in Managua

A coffee grower in Nicaragua has a nearly perfect hedge against domestic currency risk—for example, a depreciation against the dollar—because the dollar price of coffee would be unaffected by depreciation of the córdoba. Indeed, the coffee grower's profits, in both currencies, would typically rise with devaluation: in córdobas, because the córdoba prices of local inputs would rise less than the córdoba price of coffee; and in dollars, because the dollar price of coffee would stay the same while the dollar prices of inputs would fall.

So rational foreign lenders might offer Nicaraguan coffee growers a lower interest rate on foreign currency loans than they would offer the Nicaraguan government, whose tax base measured in dollars would fall with depreciation of the córdoba. But they rarely do. Problems in the legal framework for secured lending prevent potential lenders from looking beyond the farmer to the coffee. So Nicaraguan coffee growers get little credit advantage from the insulation of their collateral from macroeconomic risk. The advantage goes to importers in New Orleans or New York. There the same coffee serves as collateral for loans priced at the lowest inventory financing rates—because in those jurisdictions stocks of coffee can be readily recovered and sold to pay the debts they secure.

and sell the collateral in time to cover a debt in default. Indeed, the very same commodities, once imported into industrial countries, represent excellent collateral for loans—because in these countries the legal framework does permit the timely recovery and sale of collateral (box 2.1).

When foreign lenders do offer such loans, they typically offer them only for commodities stored in warehouses they control. While this is better than nothing, it means that producers must depend on other sources of credit for the entire growing and harvest season. Again, the issue is not macroeconomic risk. Instead, it is the poor legal framework for secured lending, which prevents potential lenders from looking beyond the producers to the internationally traded commodity.

SUPPORTING THE OBJECTIVES OF REFORM OF BANK SUPERVISION AND REGULATION

Reform focusing on supervision and regulation of banks also improves access to credit. High interest rates stem in part from large spreads between deposit and lending rates offered by banks. Improving bank supervision and regulation can often reduce these spreads, mainly by getting banks to better align their lending terms with credit risk. Reduced spreads mean greater access to credit for those with good collateral. But for those who can offer only movable property other than automobiles as collateral, they often bring no change or even worsen the terms of loans.

Reforming the legal framework for secured transactions can therefore broaden the gains from reduced spreads. By increasing the range of property that, when taken as collateral, can lower the risk of lending, it expands access to credit—either expanding the volume of lending that can be undertaken at a given interest rate or leading to lower interest rates on the existing volume of lending.[3]

Some projects to reform the financial sector and the supervision of banks aim to increase competition among banks and promote efficiency as a way to lower interest rates. A reformed law of secured transactions supports this objective by enabling nonbank financial intermediaries to better compete with banks and further drive down spreads. By allowing the use of portfolios of unsecured loans or chattel paper as collateral, the reformed law enables these intermediaries to fund their lending activities through public or private placements secured by such portfolios (called "securitization" when loans are made by issuing capital market debt secured by such collateral; see the following section).

Reforming the legal framework for secured transactions also simplifies the task of bank supervision and regulation. A sound legal framework for secured lending encourages the development of nonbank financial intermediaries that can finance their activities through securitization rather than by taking deposits, reducing the share of total credit allocated by banks. Together, these effects limit the need for government guarantees, government insurance, and bank supervision. In the United States nonbank private lenders account for about 60 percent of the credit extended; in countries whose legal framework for secured transactions is obsolete, they account for less than 5 percent. Such differences are consequential: reducing the size of the insured banking sector relative to GDP reduces the macroeconomic risk associated with the collapse of deposit-taking banks.

FOSTERING CAPITAL MARKET DEVELOPMENT

Capital markets can play an important role in development finance. They can expand competition within banking systems by allowing banks to issue loans and then move the loans off their balance sheets by selling them to outside investors—who bundle loans and use them as collateral for bonds or commercial paper in the process known as securitization. Capital markets can finance other intermediaries that compete with banks—both nonbank lenders and firms that sell on credit. And they can support firms in issuing stocks and bonds—securitized and ordinary—by giving them direct access to funds from the public. Modern systems of secured transactions form the basis for these financial operations by setting out the fundamental legal framework for securitization.

Under obsolete frameworks for secured transactions capital markets can undertake securitization and asset-based lending only under a stand-alone securitization law.[4] These laws require that investors use a riskier and more expensive system of securitization by transfer, rather than taking a security interest in a portfolio still in the hands of the original creditor. Moreover, adding one more law to the already fragmented traditional approach does not offer the reductions in risk and cost of a modern system of secured transactions, which resolves fundamental problems in priority, collection, and insulation from bankruptcy and transfer of accounts. These advances in securitization are key, particularly for encouraging nonbank lenders such as microfinance institutions, companies selling equipment on credit, and even companies extending normal 30- to 90-day credit to their clients. Under a reformed legal framework such nonbank lenders can use portfolios of loans and accounts receivable as collateral for commercial paper and bonds floated in capital markets.

While capital markets support equity finance, as a practical matter equity markets cannot substitute for legal systems that permit debt finance.[5] Equity finance plays a smaller role than debt finance. And equity markets require standards of disclosure and protection of minority shareholders far more difficult to satisfy than even the defective lending standards in place in most countries with unreformed systems of secured transactions. Even in the United States, where there has been enormous investment in the legal and regulatory infrastructure for capital markets, new equity issues represent a small fraction of total investment. In recent years new U.S. stock issues amounted to only 10 percent of new investment, while new borrowing amounted to about 40 percent.[8]

SHORING UP STATE LOAN AND GUARANTEE PROGRAMS

Following years of state-supported lending and guarantee programs that failed because of nonperforming loans, multilateral institutions have been withdrawing support and encouraging governments to privatize these state credit programs. But whether privatized or operating like private lenders, the programs can succeed only if the legal framework for debt collection is improved.

Without a change in this legal framework, these publicly subsidized programs simply transfer to governments the risks that the private sector is unwilling to take in the present legal environment. Since governments typically have no advantage in managing these risks, the risks remain high, with the consequences showing up as losses to the state lenders.

Many state lenders remain in operation because they make loans deemed socially necessary to important productive sectors of the economy. But even while they continue to operate, improving the legal framework for secured lending can support the objectives of liquidation or privatization in two ways. First, it would permit the private sector to make many of these socially necessary loans, allowing governments to reduce their involvement. Second, it would enable the state lenders to achieve their objectives with a lower loan loss rate.

ALLOWING THE GROWTH OF FINANCIAL LEASING

In otherwise unreformed legal regimes financial leasing offers an important advantage as a lending device by reducing collection costs and shortening the time required for selling collateral.[7] Using a financial lease often allows the lessor (lender) to skip the judicial process for enforcement. Since the lessor owns the leasehold collateral, the lessor can sell the collateral without the mandated judicially administered sale.

Still, financial leasing typically cannot avoid the repossession problems arising from an obsolete enforcement process. Some laws permit a lessor to recover leased property when it is on public property and its repossession will not breach the peace—for example, cars, trucks, and buses parked on public streets. But when leasehold collateral is in the possession of the lessee (debtor), the lessor still must first obtain a court order for repossession. Moreover, some sophisticated jurisdictions (such as Colombia) recognize leasing as a "simulated transaction" in which the retention of title is a device to avoid the law's provisions for recovery of the collateral—and require a court order for repossession even when it would not breach the peace. Getting a court order takes a long time, lowering the chance of repossessing the collateral and realizing much from its sale.

So leasing works best for cars, trucks, and buses. It cannot be used for inventories of untitled goods, accounts receivable, or chattel paper; nor can a lease secure a credit line. But cars, trucks, and buses amount to less than 15 percent of the movable capital stock in most countries, limiting the extent of leasing. Moreover, tax difficulties often arise because the lessee must pay taxes when the lessor purchases the leasehold property and again when the property is transferred to the lessee. Leasing therefore tends to focus on new goods, amounting to only about 1.5 percent of the movable capital stock.

Thus while financial leasing offers clear benefits even in an unreformed framework for security interests, a reform that addresses the most severe faults of that framework would strengthen financial leasing and increase its economic impact. In particular, a reformed legal system would permit the bundling of leases into portfolios that can serve as collateral for refinancing loans from other lenders. Such private and public securitizations would provide financing that would allow lessors (such as leasing companies) to expand their operations.

SUPPORTING JUDICIAL REFORM

Judicial reform has many important public policy justifications. Further justification might appear to be the long, judicially administered procedures for debt collection that limit access to credit because they limit the economic value of collateral.

But modern systems have speeded debt collection largely by removing it from the courts rather than by trying to reform them. Repossession and sale of collateral occur largely without judicial intervention. Instead, they are undertaken under the control of the creditor, which is subject to penalties for abuse. Judicial reform is unlikely to match the speed of private collection. Even in advanced industrial countries with modern judiciaries, completing a civil suit can take one to three years—far too long to allow perishable or rapidly depreciating movable property to serve as collateral.

Of course, when debtors are intransigent and private methods of seizure and sale fail, the creditor may need a court order to instruct the police or other state enforcement agent to forcibly repossess the collateral. But a well-designed modern law gives the judge no discretion in issuing that order. Instead, the judge must issue it upon receiving evidence that the debt has not been paid, even if the debtor is not present. Such a law, requiring a simple decision, can operate well even in judicial regimes otherwise in need of substantial reform. Debtors in such systems do not forgo their defenses against unfair collection, but they cannot use them to prevent repossession.

Although judicial reform is not necessary for a modern secured transactions system, a modern secured transactions system can offer substantial support to judicial reform. In many countries a large share of court cases involve debt collection, and in countries that still practice debt imprisonment a large share of inmates are in jail for unpaid debts. A reformed system for secured transactions can reduce burdens on courts and prisons, freeing judicial systems to focus on administering justice.

REINFORCING THE STRENGTHS OF MICROFINANCE INSTITUTIONS

Supporting the development of the microfinance industry has been a key item on multilateral and bilateral donors' agenda for expanding access to finance. Microfinance institutions, through innovations in lending technologies, have created profitable financial services for the poor and underserved, greatly expanding access to credit. Many of these institutions have become key players in the financial sector (such as BRI Indonesia, ProCredit Bank in Albania, and Banco Solidario, or BancoSol, in Bolivia). In many low- and middle-income countries these lenders compete for the same clients as commercial banks and have even become licensed commercial banks themselves.

Microfinance institutions have achieved all that in environments with poor legal frameworks, including those for secured lending. Yet it would be a mistake to assume that they would not benefit from reforms in the legal framework for secured transactions. Although microfinance institutions rely on substitutes for collateral (peer pressure, access to repeat loans, innovative—and sometimes illegal—enforcement mechanisms), reforming collateral laws may have a greater effect on them than on conventional banks. The reason? The movable property and fixtures that reform newly permits borrowers to use as collateral tend to be a better match for the property owned by microfinance clients, who do not own real estate on the same scale as borrowers from the formal sector. Indeed, anecdotal evidence suggests that in some countries that have undertaken secured transactions reform, the initial uptake in using the system for registering security interests was bigger among microfinance institutions than among commercial banks.[8] And microfinance institutions—like all other lenders—will provide larger loans (relative to cash flow), lower interest rates, and longer maturities for loans secured by property than for unsecured loans (see the discussion of BancoSol in chapter 1).

Microfinance institutions would also benefit from the effect of the reform on unsecured lending. Gathering information about unsecured borrowers can be expensive and difficult, but lenders and sellers on credit often do so anyway in the course of dealing with their clients over the years. The information they acquire can be quite valuable, allowing them to make unsecured loans and extend unsecured credit inexpensively and profitably. But fully realizing the value of this information requires a reformed system for secured transactions that permits refinancing the portfolios of unsecured loans that microfinance lenders hold.

Inability to refinance such portfolios has limited the expansion of small, pioneering unsecured lenders, including solidarity-group lenders. But where a framework for secured transactions supports securitization, permitting the refinancing of small unsecured loans by businesses that do not take deposits, it reduces the cost of unsecured lending and promotes the development of non-bank competition. In the United States, for example, large finance companies such as American Express, Diners Club, and MBNA make unsecured loans, then use portfolios of these loans as collateral for their own loans and issues of commercial paper. The consequences for nonbank competition are clear: as noted, while in most developing countries nonbank credit amounts to about 5 percent of total credit, in the United States it amounts to about 60 percent of the total.

NOTES

1. Heywood Fleisig and Nuria de la Peña, "Should the Bank and the Fund Support the Reform of Secured Transactions?" CEAL Issues Brief (Center for the Economic Analysis of Law, Washington, D.C., 2003).

2. Only rarely will a bank make a local currency loan at a lower interest rate to a private borrower than to the government. The local government's ability to tax and to print local currency means that government debt denominated in local currency will typically have a lower risk and therefore a lower interest rate.

3. E. Gerald Corrigan, formerly president of the Federal Reserve Bank of New York and now a managing director of Goldman Sachs, discusses the links between the legal system and bank supervision and regulation clearly and accessibly in an article on Latin America and the Caribbean, stating that "the region's credit problems ... *will not* [emphasis in original] be solved simply by improved supervisory policies and practices" ("Building Effective Banking Systems in Latin America and the

Caribbean: Tactics and Strategy," IFM-107 (Inter-American Development Bank, Washington, D.C., 1997, p. 14). While the article focuses on Latin America, it applies equally well to bank supervision and regulation in all developing countries.

4. See chapter 3 for a detailed discussion of the legal roots of this problem.

5. Equity finance theoretically could replace debt finance: the two are interchangeable at the margin. Consequently, it could be argued that a viable project that is not financed with borrowing would be financed by equity investment. If that were the case, a poor framework for secured lending would only shift the balance of financing away from debt and toward equity. In that view a defective system of secured transactions would have no overall economic cost: either debt or equity would eventually finance all profitable projects. This argument appears only in the legal literature, not in the economics literature, and appears to have been first suggested by Alan Schwartz, in "The Continuing Puzzle of Secured Debt" (*Vanderbilt Law Review* 37 [October 1984]: 1051–69). This article, followed in the legal literature by a long debate on its merits, rests on a subtle fallacy familiar to economists: that equality at the margin implies equality on inframarginal transactions. By the same false logic one could claim to show that since imported and domestically produced goods are equal in price at the margin, no incentive for trade exists; or that because the rate of return on the marginal project equals the interest rate, no profit would arise from positive investment.

6. From 2000 to mid-2005 U.S. business invested $1.1 trillion a year on average. Average annual stock issues amounted to about $120 billion, a little over 10 percent of the total; average annual borrowing from the financial sector amounted to $425 billion, about 40 percent of the total. See U.S. Federal Reserve System, Board of Governors, *Flow of Funds Accounts of the United States: Flows and Outstandings, Second Quarter 2005,* Federal Reserve Statistical Release Z.1 (Washington, D.C., 2005), p. 17.

7. Donors, especially the International Finance Corporation through its Private Enterprise Partnerships, have strongly supported reforms of leasing laws. The partnerships have worked on such reforms in Kazakhstan, the Kyrgyz Republic, FYR Macedonia, and Ukraine and are now expanding to several countries in Africa.

8. This is based on conversations with stakeholders in Albania and Bosnia and Herzegovina.

CHAPTER 3

THE ECONOMIC CONSEQUENCES OF OBSOLETE SYSTEMS FOR SECURED TRANSACTIONS

Obsolete laws governing secured transactions make it difficult to use property as collateral, raising hurdles in each stage of the process—creation, priority, publicity, and enforcement of a security interest. Lawyers in countries considering reform of secured transactions systems are unlikely to know how different features of their law restrict the use of collateral and thus limit access to credit. Nor are other stakeholders likely to know that these limits on access to credit, often central to their policy and business concerns, stem from defects in the law. It is the job of task managers and project teams to explain how these defects limit access to credit—and to do so throughout the reform process, from justifying this reform against other possible financial sector reforms, to motivating government ministers and members of parliament.

This chapter sets out examples of legal problems in each stage of obsolete systems and outlines their economic consequences. For many readers the chapter may (necessarily) require the mastery of some new terms. While not daunting, this requirement does underscore the need for reform projects to have continual advice from a lawyer well versed in the operation of modern (or reformed) systems for secured transactions.

CREATION: PROBLEMS THAT EXCLUDE GOODS, AGENTS, AND TRANSACTIONS

Many legal systems place needless restrictions on creating security interests, excluding economically important property, agents, and transactions. Where such gaps exist, lenders cannot be sure that a secured transaction, such as a loan agreement using collateral (a security agreement), will be lawful and that a court will enforce it. Special statutes authorizing the creation of security interests in movable property may restrict the parties able to undertake the transaction, the nature of the transaction, and the type of property that can serve as collateral. Under this fragmented approach a law may have limited application: Some laws may apply only to banks, registered businesses, consumers, microenterprises, or farmers. Some may apply only to pledges, leases, mortgages, trust agreements, or sales with retention of title. And some may apply only to cattle or mining equipment. The end result is that some loans cannot be secured with movable property, some property cannot secure a loan, and some borrowers and lenders cannot use some types of instruments or give or take a security interest in some types of property.

LIMITS ON WHO CAN BE A PARTY TO A SECURITY AGREEMENT

Unreformed systems place restrictions on who can be a party to a security agreement and thus limit who can lend and who can borrow. Sometimes such restrictions serve no public policy purpose, as when farmers cannot give a security interest in their property to merchants.[1] Sometimes they undermine good public policy, as when a woman cannot sign a security agreement—or when only corporations can file security interests in the company registry, a restriction excluding most farmers, all microenterprises, and most small and medium-size ones (box 3.1). Sometimes they are side effects of apparently unrelated laws, as when laws set the minimum age for signing a contract above the age of many heads of household, particularly among the poor.

BOX 3.1

The intricacies of law can shut many out of the formal market

In Mexico a recent attempt to reform the system for secured transactions focused on the commercial pledge, *prenda mercantil.* Support for this work came from the agriculture divisions of the World Bank and the Inter-American Development Bank, signifying its perceived importance for farmers. But because small farmers do not qualify as commercial entities under Mexico's civil code, it is unclear whether they are bound by the commercial code. That leaves room for doubt that a commercial pledge signed by a farmer is legally valid, a legal risk that minimized the reform's effect on agriculture.

In Bangladesh, India, and Jamaica a company can give a security interest—a "charge"—against all its property, movable and immovable. But that charge must be filed in the company registry, which deals only with corporations (companies). This system for publicity of security interests thus excludes the sole proprietorships that make up the vast majority of enterprises in these countries—all microenterprises and many small and medium-size ones.

Such restrictions sometimes affect a large share of the population, such as when all farmers cannot use collateral. And they sometimes have a disproportionate effect on groups targeted by donors, such as women or poor people. The greater the potential economic importance of the groups affected, the greater the economic impact of the limits on their access to credit.

LIMITS ON COVERAGE OF GOODS AND TRANSACTIONS

Traditional systems often limit the coverage of goods and transactions. Laws may exclude from the realm of collateral several types of assets—goods that do not yet exist, such as a future crop; goods that lack a title; intangible assets representing rights to other property, such as copyrights, air rights, or accounts receivable; or fixtures, movable property subsequently affixed to immovable property, such as a silo, an oven, an escalator, or a central air conditioning system. Some laws apply to pledges of a particular item, such as cattle. Others may limit or exclude transactions, such as a second-priority security interest (box 3.2).

This spotty coverage creates two economic problems. First, when assets cannot serve as collateral, the owners of those assets cannot get the benefit of

---

BOX 3.2

How to protect first-priority lenders while preserving competition

As borrowers accumulate equity—as they pay off a first creditor or as the value of an asset pledged as collateral increases—they might wish to finance a second-priority security interest with a competing lender. In Bangladesh, however, the law restricts security interests to one per item of collateral. And in Bolivia the pledge law does not void an agreement that requires the permission of the first-priority lender for the borrower to give a second-priority security interest to another creditor. These restrictions are aimed at strengthening the position of the first-priority creditor. But they do so at the cost of greatly restricting competition and giving the first-priority creditor monopoly power over the debtor. Moreover, under rules like these, financing methods such as second-mortgage home equity lines of credit cannot be developed. Modern systems void any agreements that include restrictions on granting other creditors a second-priority security interest and protect the first-priority creditor by giving that creditor power to control the sale of collateral, even if the debtor defaults on the loan of a lower-priority creditor. This rule protects the first-priority creditor without sacrificing competition among lenders.

---

secured lending. Consider the consequences of laws in civil code countries that treat fixtures as part of the real estate to which they are attached and grant real estate mortgages "superpriority" to include any fixtures on the property: If a business operator wanting to finance a fixture owns the building, the operator must go to the expense of refinancing the entire mortgage. If the business operator rents the building, no lender will finance the fixture because the holder of the mortgage on the real estate would have first claim on the fixture (see the section in this chapter on limits on creating security interests in fixtures).

Moreover, these complex and arbitrary divisions can diminish the use of property as collateral simply by creating confusion about what is included under the law. In Nicaragua a law that permits taking a security interest in a future crop, for example, limits such interests to crops that will be harvested within 18 months. This excludes most forestry financing. Moreover, if a natural disaster should destroy this year's crop, the requirement limits continuation of the pledge in crop in the following years. Where such uncertainty exists, lenders know that a lawsuit may be needed to clarify matters if a borrower defaults. So lenders typically avoid such risks by giving little weight in the lending decision to property whose use as collateral is questionable.

Second, transaction costs rise when much time and effort must be devoted to determining whether the law permits taking a security interest in a particular item. In Peru fish meal can be pledged as collateral because it can meet Peru's legal requirements for specific identification through the identification number stenciled onto each pallet. But fruit concentrate, stored in containers of no standard size and with no identification, cannot meet those requirements and so cannot serve as collateral. In Argentina wine in barrels kept in field warehouses—storage units supervised by lenders—can serve as collateral because each barrel can be separately identified. But grain in silos, not so identified, cannot serve as collateral. These distinctions serve no public policy purpose. And they can be painful and costly to those who learn about them through the expensive process of losing a court case.

LIMITS ON USING A GENERAL DESCRIPTION OF COLLATERAL OR A FLOATING SECURITY INTEREST

Under a traditional approach a security agreement, to be valid, must specifically identify collateral (such as each item of an inventory) rather than describe the collateral in general terms (box 3.3). This requirement follows from the model of mortgages on real estate, where specific identification is important

BOX 3.3

Can a future crop serve as collateral?

As a case in Nicaragua shows, unreformed laws specifying what can serve as collateral can accidentally exclude important goods. Recognizing the potential importance of being able to pledge future crops, Nicaragua included an agricultural pledge of future crop in its civil code early in the 20th century. Later, when crop exports became important, borrowers attempted to pledge future crops under the framework of that code, only to find that they often could not comply with the legal requirement to fully describe in detail the crop that was going to be harvested. Of course, there is no public policy reason why borrowers should not be able to pledge a broad description of a future crop. The problem arises entirely from the narrowly drafted law and the court's otherwise reasonable desire not to stretch the scope of laws beyond their demonstrable legislative intent.

in identifying collateral so that unsecured creditors may rely on the debtor's other assets.

The requirement for specific identification can raise the costs of creating a security interest to prohibitive levels. Some goods are well identified. Well-developed systems of registration, enforced by police, typically exist for such property as ships, planes, and automobiles, making them relatively easy to identify. But most movable property is difficult to identify with precision. While some consumer and producer goods have serial numbers, these numbers may be easily removed or changed and records are rarely kept. Other movable goods have no specific identification: grain, petroleum, canned goods in a warehouse, nuts and bolts.

Requiring specific identification can also increase risk, by making loans harder to monitor. A $10,000 loan secured by the inventory of an appliance store can be monitored easily by visiting the store. But if the security agreement cites specific serial numbers, it is not enough for the loan officer to confirm that the store has sufficient inventory; the loan officer must determine whether the specific appliances mentioned in the agreement are on the floor. And consider the difference in monitoring costs between visually counting, say, refrigerators and turning every one around to check its serial number.

In not permitting general descriptions, unreformed systems raise a costly and sometimes conceptually insurmountable barrier to the finance of inventories and accounts receivable, which together are about as big as the entire

BOX 3.4

Was the lender fleeced?
Why the wool in the rug is not the wool in the bale

In Uruguay, where wool is a major export, the good is in principle excellent collateral for either a peso or a dollar loan. It has a standard international grade, is traded in international markets, and has a long storage life. If the Uruguayan peso depreciated, the dollar price of wool would remain roughly unchanged while the peso price would rise. For these reasons Uruguayan banks willingly made loans secured by wool stored in warehouses. According to a Central Bank official, speaking at a 1995 Central Bank seminar on secured transactions in Montevideo, a problem arose in the late 1980s when a borrower failed to make the payments due and the bank went to foreclose. The borrower asserted that the wool in the warehouse was not the wool pledged to the bank: "Your wool is gone—it is in sweaters, in rugs. This wool is pledged to another lender." The bank argued that this was absurd, that the bank had renewed for years a loan secured by the firm's wool inventory, wherever it might be found and in whatever state. But the court ruled in favor of the borrower. It noted that each bale of wool had an identification number stenciled on it. The bank should have kept track of these numbers and rewritten the pledge each time the wool rotated—a requirement that increased monitoring costs enormously. The effect? A decline in financing wool.

stock of movable equipment held by business. Limiting the enforceability of security interests to collateral that has been specifically identified means that a security interest in general inventories, such as wheat or appliances, cannot "float" to new inventories once the original goods have been sold (box 3.4). A similar problem arises with accounts receivable.

Businesses hold inventory for the precise purpose of turning it over. If the law does not permit the security interest to float, secured by generally described homogeneous property such as inventory and accounts receivable, such property cannot serve as security for a line of credit. A lender would fear, correctly, that the security interest would disappear when the goods are sold. This conflicts with the economic fact that the debtor aims to sell the inventory—indeed, must sell it to stay in business and service the debt. A lender faces a similar predicament when offered a portfolio of accounts receivable as collateral. All parties want the accounts receivable to be paid—to allow the debtor to buy more inventory to sell and generate more accounts receivable. If the security interest cannot float to new inventory and the new accounts entering the portfolio, the accounts would be worthless as collateral. Knowing this, rational lenders in unreformed systems do not finance inventory and accounts receivable.

Modern laws avoid this problem. They permit using property of any type as the object of a security agreement with the exception of exclusions that are specifically listed.[2] This broad structure permits a security agreement to describe the collateral in whatever way the secured party and borrower deem appropriate. For example, an agreement might describe a quantity ("300 head of Hereford cattle") or a specific identification ("Roger Prime Blue Ribbon, Hereford bull, tattoo #123, breeding registry #456").

Modern laws thus permit security interests to float on broadly defined stocks of goods serving as inventory, or on accounts receivable or chattel paper in a portfolio. Moreover, the priority of the security interests does not change as the inventory and accounts receivable revolve.

LIMITS ON CREATING A SECURITY INTEREST IN AFTER-ACQUIRED COLLATERAL OR AFTER-CREATED DEBT

Unreformed systems often permit the pledging only of collateral that presently exists ("present collateral"). This rule evolved from early ideas that a thing that did not exist could not be pledged. While this restriction may appear innocuous, it has a large adverse economic effect.

The essence of economic activity lies in transforming that which exists—seeds, cotton, steel—into that which does not yet exist—food, clothes, machines. During that transformation producers need working capital. In particular, they need financing for the labor input. That labor is embodied in the output, not the material input. Providing sufficient collateral for working capital therefore requires the security offered by the output, not yet created, rather than the input. A law that prevents taking such property as collateral chokes off the supply of working capital. Unreformed systems sometimes take modest steps to address this problem by permitting specific pledges for certain kinds of after-acquired collateral, such as a crop in the field. But no successful strategy can depend on the specific enumeration of all possible transformations: there are too many possible transformations, and producers constantly invent new ones.

Similar problems arise from another apparently harmless and reasonable requirement: that borrowers own the property offered as collateral before they can grant security interests in it. But in the normal course of trade borrowers need to finance things they do not own. Exporters need working capital secured by promises to pay in order to start working on their next order. Importers need credit to pay for goods that they will not "own" until these goods arrive in the country. To finance these exports and imports, lenders will want to know what their priority will be at the instant the exporter receives the promise of payment or the importer becomes the owner. Laws that prevent taking such security interests effectively prevent the financing of trade. Donors' attempts to fill this gap with state-guaranteed credit lines (such as preexport facilities) turn a legal problem that is simple to solve into a risky unsecured lending scheme.

Modern secured transactions systems permit all property, whether existing or to be acquired in the future, to serve as collateral for a loan. That permits a lender to finance farmers before they plant a crop or manufacturers before they create output. Moreover, the lender is assured that the security interest in that output is well defined under the law and can take a first priority through-out the production process. There is no need to enter into a new security agreement each time new goods come into the inventory, facilitating the rotation of inventory and the financing of farming.

Modern systems also permit property not "owned" by the borrower to serve as collateral for a loan. They leave it up to the lender to determine whether property rights other than ownership that a borrower may acquire in an asset are sufficiently valuable and transferable to serve as collateral.

PRIORITY: PROBLEMS THAT UNDERMINE LENDERS' SECURITY

A key feature distinguishing secured from unsecured lending lies in the ability of a secured lender to establish a ranking among those who might have a claim against property offered as collateral. Clear rules for establishing priority among creditors permit lenders to assess a loan's potential risk and return based on its size, the value of collateral, and the order of priority of other creditors.

With rules for establishing priority, a lender can determine the value of a borrower's assets as collateral—as opposed to their market value—because the lender can discover what prior interests exist in the property. For example, an asset with a market value of $100,000 might provide sufficient collateral for a loan of $30,000 if there are no prior security interests, but not if there is a prior security interest of $90,000.

Rules for establishing priority among creditors also increase the likelihood that a secured lender will recover the value of collateral. An unsecured lender can go to court to enforce an unsecured loan and get a judgment lien that calls for seizing the property of the debtor and selling it to satisfy the debt. Typically, though, that judgment lien will have lower priority than an existing loan properly secured by the debtor's property. Even if there is no prior security interest, the unsecured lender has to worry that another unsecured lender will take an earlier court action, have the property seized and sold, and be paid first, leaving nothing for other unsecured creditors. Or the debtor may declare bankruptcy, with the result that payments are assigned by a bankruptcy court and the unsecured lender recovers only a fraction of the debt.

Unreformed systems, however, offer unclear guidance about priority. Different security interest laws may have different priority structures, creating confusion about the order of priority. For example, if a debtor pledges property that the debtor leased, who prevails—the lender or the lessor? Moreover, laws may give superpriority to some creditors—such as the state, on tax liens—allowing them priority over existing security interests that had been filed in the registry before these creditors made their claims. When priority rules contradict one another, they compound lenders' uncertainty and thus lower the value of property as collateral.

The coexistence of different systems of priority can also create uncertainty. One system of priority is based on the possessory security interest, where the collateral is given to the lender. Priority comes through possession. This simple system, one of the oldest for securing loans with movable property, governs pawnshops, gold and silver loans, and most warehousing systems operating under unreformed laws. Since the creditor's possession of the collateral is open and public, the transaction protects other potential lenders. If a borrower offers a lender as collateral a watch in the possession of a pawnshop, for example, the prospective lender would naturally suspect that the watch secures a prior loan.

Unreformed laws are often silent on the contradiction that might arise if a borrower who has given a security interest in goods under a nonpossessory system then transfers them to a possessory system. Suppose, for example, that a miller has given a security interest in wheat held in its storeroom, but then moves that wheat to a warehouse and offers the warehouse receipt as collateral for another loan. Does the nonpossessory security interest in the wheat have priority over the possessory security of the lender secured by the warehouse receipt (box 3.5)? Like multiple laws, multiple systems with inconsistent priority rules diminish the value of priority for all property.

BOX 3.5

Muddy priority sinks the pledge of the future crop

Some countries (such as Nicaragua and Romania before reform) have laws permitting the pledge of a future crop. Drafters perceived, correctly, that this instrument could expand access to credit for farmers.

The priority for pledges of a future crop is determined by the time of filing in the real estate archive. But some of these countries also have warehouse laws that give priority in the goods in a warehouse to its operator. By establishing a clear priority rule for the warehouse, these laws too expand access to credit, for farmers who have stored their harvest. This priority rule is harmless as long as it applies only to the storage costs charged by the warehouse operator. Under some systems, however, it extends to the warehouse receipt and the use of that receipt as collateral for a loan.

So, who has priority if a farmer harvests a crop that had been pledged, puts that pledged crop in a warehouse, and then uses the warehouse receipt as collateral for another loan? The lender to whom the future crop had been pledged or the warehouse operator? Unclear. Because of this uncertainty lenders will not lend against a future crop, and the risk in warehousing is needlessly raised.

Modern systems integrate the priorities under all security laws and other possible claims against property into a single first-to-file priority system. So for nearly all security devices priority is determined by the time of filing in the filing archive (see the section in this chapter on publicity).[3] Creating a common system for priority across all laws that effectively allow the taking of property as security—the comprehensive functional approach—resolves priority conflicts.

NO PRIORITY RULES FOR FUTURE ADVANCES

Unreformed systems often provide no clear priority rules for future advances—advances of funds that a creditor will make in the future, secured by the same property as an initial advance made when the security agreement is executed. Unreformed systems give a secured creditor priority for the initial advance. But they do not extend this priority to subsequent payments and drawings on the account secured by that security interest.

This legal structure makes it impossible for lenders to safely offer revolving credit lines to borrowers. Correctly applied, the unreformed law would permit a borrower to pay off a credit line that had first priority, take out a new loan secured with the same collateral, and then draw again on the credit line. This transaction, a future advance against the credit line, would place the first lender in second position even though that lender had filed first. Lenders, understanding this, do not offer secured loans as lines of credit. Consequently, borrowers miss out on access to inexpensive revolving credit lines.

Reformed systems address this problem by setting out priority rules for future advances. These rules give priority to a loan secured by particular property and assign the same priority to all future drawings against that credit line. Most modern systems balance the right of first-priority lenders to offer secured credit lines with the need to have competition from second-priority lenders by giving borrowers the right to request a limit on the amount of a credit line secured with first priority. That means that lenders can safely assess the remaining equity value in collateral before offering a second-priority secured loan. Clear laws on this issue can have large effects on credit markets. In the United States, for example, this legal structure has allowed the enormous growth of second-trust home equity lines of credit.

LIMITS ON THE CONTINUATION IN PROCEEDS AND PRODUCTS OF A SECURITY INTEREST

Unreformed systems often permit a security interest to continue in proceeds only in a very limited way. So, for example, if a borrower sells a specific piece of equipment serving as collateral and does not replace it with new equipment, the object of the security interest disappears. Of course, having sold the equipment, the borrower now has cash. But under unreformed systems the security interest in the equipment does not automatically carry over to the cash. Moreover, civil code jurisdictions that permit continuation in proceeds define proceeds as the "fruits and products" of the original collateral. This definition is very limited because it includes only the first disposition of the collateral and no subsequent dispositions. For example, if the collateral is a specifically identified standing crop, the pledge will automatically continue against the grain from the standing crop. But it will not continue against the cash deposited in a bank account from the sale of the grain, or against the next crop or the tractor financed with that cash. If a tax lien or other claim were to attach against a debtor's cash deposits and future crop and tractor financed from the sale of the original collateral, the secured creditor could not collect first against any of these other assets.

These limits on the continuation in proceeds pose a major risk to the lender. Once the chain of security interest is broken, the lender must negotiate a new security interest in the proceeds or products of the original collateral. If the borrower refuses to negotiate a new agreement, the lender must turn to the court to collect. Even if the lender prevails, the claim will not have the priority of the original security interest. Instead, it will be treated like an unsecured claim in default.

This approach imposes costs on lenders through delay and court costs and through the greater chance of losing priority to another lender that might obtain a security interest in the proceeds or goods into which the debtor has transformed the original collateral. Lenders can guard against these adverse outcomes through greater vigilance, but such vigilance is also costly—especially with borrowers whose equipment or crop naturally turns over rapidly in the course of trade. For lenders the limits on continuation in proceeds raises transaction costs and risk. For borrowers these limits produce higher interest rates and smaller loans relative to their cash flow and the value of their collateral.

In modern systems a security interest can continue in proceeds for an indefinite period or number of transactions, limited only by the ability to trace those proceeds. With continuation in proceeds, lenders can be more confident of retaining their original priority. Modern systems include, of course, the direct transformations into fruits and products, such as cows into calves and seed into crops. But they also include economic transformations, such as the transformation of the grain into cash or that of the cash into a car. During the period of transformation the security interest would automatically attach to the cash received (continue in the proceeds) from the sale or to the car purchased with the cash.

The lender can also obtain, without further court intervention, the assistance of other private agents in the collection of the debt. The borrower, knowing this, is less tempted to avoid payment or settlement.

LIMITS ON CREATING SECURITY INTERESTS IN FIXTURES
As noted, a fixture is previously movable property that has been physically attached to real estate. Fixtures include economically important classes of equipment—such as ovens, generators, elevators, water pumps, freezing chambers, and construction cranes.

Many unreformed legal systems treat such equipment as movable property until it is affixed to real estate, when they begin treating it as part of the land or building. So at the moment it is affixed the fixture moves from the legal regime governing movable property to the regime governing real estate. Then its financing is subject to the combined problems in financing each type of property.

BOX 3.6

Burning dollars

When the government of Romania privatized a large bakery by turning it over to its workers and managers, one of the first challenges the new owners faced was the obsolete equipment. The manager said, "This oven is so inefficient that when you turn it on, it's not like baking bread, it's like burning dollars." Under modern systems for secured transactions many manufacturers sell such equipment to firms on credit, repossessing it if a firm fails to pay. But because Romanian law treated equipment as part of the building to which it is attached, any firm that sold an oven to the bakery would have transferred ownership to the government—which still owned the building—rather than retained it as collateral for a loan.

Under unreformed systems, once equipment pledged as collateral is attached to real estate, it typically becomes subject to any mortgage against that real estate.[4] Creditors with a security interest in the fixture then lose their security to mortgagee creditors secured by the real estate.

Attempting to surmount this problem by financing fixtures with a mortgage usually creates new difficulties. This strategy represents no solution, of course, where the borrower is only renting the property to which the fixture will be attached (box 3.6). Even where the borrower owns the real estate, however, the merging of fixtures with real estate presents problems for financing. Often only one mortgage per property is valid, so the borrower must incur the cost of refinancing the entire mortgage just to finance the fixture. Where second mortgages are permitted, high notarization costs make the financing very costly. Moreover, in transition economies where state farms cannot be sold or transferred, or under agrarian reform regimes that prohibit small farmers or cooperatives from selling or leasing land received under the reform, the legal status of a security interest that finances fixtures and structures is unclear. This uncertainty raises the risk of lending secured by such collateral.

Even if a mortgage is used to secure an interest in a fixture, enforcement of mortgages typically takes just as long as enforcement against movable property, generally one to three years—by which time fixtures could depreciate and deteriorate enormously. Moreover, unreformed mortgage laws often do not clearly specify the ability of the new owner, after foreclosing on real estate collateral, to evict the debtor.

Because of this mixing of the legal frameworks for movable and immovable property, no rational lender will finance the purchase or sale on credit of a fixture without also having a first mortgage on the real estate to which it is or will be attached. This represents a severe constraint on financing, as many leasing and finance companies would be ready to finance the equipment that will be affixed to real estate, but uninterested in a mortgage on the real estate.

Reformed systems separate the framework for securing loans with movable property and fixtures from the framework for mortgaging the principal real estate. This separation, by reducing the risks and transaction costs of financing heavy equipment, produces a key economic benefit.

HIDDEN TAX LIABILITIES AND SUPERPRIORITY FOR THE STATE

Unreformed systems for perfecting security interests typically either fail to set out clear rules for ranking the priority of a security interest relative to tax claims or give a clear superpriority to tax claims. Under such a system the law might grant secured creditors a ranking of priority based on the date they filed their security interest in the registry. But another law might give the state priority for taxes due regardless of when or even whether the state filed a tax lien against the property serving as collateral.

When the state's claims are not public, a potential lender cannot tell in advance whether property offered as collateral has tax claims against it. Because the lender's right against the collateral depends on a fact that is difficult for the lender to know—whether the borrower has any hidden tax liability—such systems undermine the purpose of collateral.

Similar problems arise from giving superpriority to debts to the state, including loan payments due state-run banks. Superpriority allows the state to execute judgment liens against the debtor's property ahead of the security interests of private creditors, even when those state liens were filed later than the security interests or not filed at all. This fatally undercuts the secured lending system because private lenders will have no good way of determining whether a borrower has or will have unpaid tax bills or debts to state banks.

Reformed systems assign priority by the time of filing in the archive, whether for a voluntary agreement such as a security agreement or for an involuntary claim such as a tax lien or a judgment lien of a state lender for an unpaid loan. Tax authorities who argue that this approach would reduce their revenue would do better to speed up their tax collection and filing of tax liens than to undercut the lending system—because a system that enhances commerce will ultimately produce more tax revenue.

BOX 3.7

Filing archives and registries: where less is more

Bulgaria's secured transactions law, before its reform, called for filing pledges in notarial registries. With hundreds of notaries, no Bulgarian lender had any hope of discovering prior security interests. The reform introduced one central archive.

Once Bulgaria completed its reform, Peru moved up in the ranks of countries with the most registries—with 32. Each registry had been established by a different law defining a particular type of security interest, raising vexing juridical questions. For example, should the pledge of a fishing company's boat be registered in the boat registry, the company registry, or the registry of inventory? And if more than one pledge is filed in more than one place, which has priority? Even if lenders had to worry about only two registrations, the 32 registries represent nearly 500 different priority problems. Here it is the poorly drafted laws that create the greater legal uncertainty, not the multitude of registries.

DIVIDED REGISTRATION SYSTEMS THAT CAUSE CONFLICTS IN PRIORITY RULES

Unreformed systems typically do not provide a comprehensive set of priority rules covering all secured transactions. As a result, registration in separate, unlinked registries could establish priority for competing claims against the same collateral. This could happen, for example, if the leasing law calls for registration in a different system than the one in which pledges are registered.[5] Or if a security interest against an enterprise might be registered in the commercial registry while a pledge of a future crop might be registered in a real estate registry (box 3.7).

This complexity and ambiguity arising from inconsistent laws increase the risks and costs of secured lending, including financial leasing, because potential lenders that wish to take property as collateral must check more than one system to learn of an existing lease, trust, lien, or other encumbrance against the collateral. And when encumbrances are found in different registries, the laws may be silent or in conflict with one another on which registration has priority.

Reformed systems apply one system of priorities to all security interests as well as to all other transactions undertaken for purposes of security, including leases, consignments, trust agreements, and conditional sales. To ensure that priorities are unambiguous, the law generally specifies that priority is determined by the time of filing in a single filing archive.

PUBLICITY: PROBLEMS THAT HAMPER FILING OR RETRIEVAL OF RECORDS OF SECURITY INTERESTS

In any priority system that uses the filing or registration of a notice of security interest to establish priority, there must be a place or means for making the security interest public. Otherwise a lender has no practical way to determine whether prior interests in property exist when advancing credit secured by that property. Many methods of publicity have been used over the years, including public announcements, newspaper advertisements, and other public postings. The two systems in use today are the registry and, the most modern one, the notice filing archive. While registry systems file copies of the security agreement or a detailed abstract of it, notice filing archives file only a notice of its existence. Notice filing systems today are usually Internet based and allow any potential lender to quickly determine whether the property being offered as collateral by a borrower has prior security interests or other encumbrances. The registries in unreformed systems raise barriers to filing and accessing registered information, mainly through the requirements that the law places on the registration process. These requirements typically have no public policy justification that outweighs their social cost.

RESTRICTIONS ON ACCESS TO REGISTRY RECORDS

In most countries with unreformed systems the registry (or judge's office) tends to collect long lines of people waiting to get a certificate attesting to the existence of security interests or other encumbrances. Lenders often may not inspect the registry records directly.

Besides restricting who may inspect the registry records, the registry law might even restrict who may approach the registry authorities for information: sometimes only the owner of the collateral may do so, and sometimes only individuals whom the judge deems to have a "legitimate interest." Often there is no internal or external computer access to the registry. And those wishing to conduct a search need the permission of a judge or another administrative official to do so.

Lack of public access to information in the registry nullifies the intended economic effect of the priority system: if lenders cannot learn of the existence of prior encumbrances nor assert their position against collateral, they will not lend. Where registries are based on courts or notaries, determining priority can be practically impossible.

In reformed systems security interests and other encumbrances are publicized by filing a simple notice of the interest in a public filing archive. The most modern systems provide Internet access to a computer database. Anyone can search these systems by any characteristic of lender, debtor, or collateral.

REQUIREMENT FOR INSPECTION OF DOCUMENTS

Unreformed laws often require that security agreements go through several levels of clearance by state or state-appointed authorities during the registration process. They may require that security agreements be prepared by a notary. And they may require that the public registry have staffs of lawyers who inspect security agreements for legal validity. These procedures take time and cost money yet add little to lenders' security, since neither the notary nor the registry takes any financial responsibility for remaining errors.

Modern systems reason that the contracting parties should take responsibility for the legal validity of their documents; after all, they have the most to gain from getting them right. Rather than requiring state and notary certifications, laws ideally should permit their use only when the contracting parties desire.

REQUIREMENT FOR FILING DOCUMENTS RATHER THAN SIMPLY NOTICES

Unreformed laws require that the registry file the security agreement or a summary of it that the registry prepares. That raises costs and introduces substantial risk of error.

Modern notice filing systems do not file the entire agreement or even a substantial extract. Instead, they file only minimal information about the security interest—a notice of its existence that typically includes only the names and addresses of the parties, a description of the collateral, and the date and time of filing. Filing less information eases concerns about allowing greater public access to the filing system, lowers filing costs, and simplifies the registration system. Of course, this abbreviated information may not tell a potential lender enough to decide whether to accept a potential borrower's property as collateral. But the notice filing system gives the lender the information needed to inquire privately about additional details in loan contracts. If potential borrowers refuse to supply that information, lenders are free to refuse their loan application.

MULTIPLE AND UNLINKED REGISTRIES

Unreformed systems often have multiple registries—separate registries for different geographic areas, types of collateral, types of transaction, types of filing entity, jurisdictions of law, or supervising ministries. These registries are typically unlinked. Even where the law is clear about priority, the multiplicity of registries often can make search practically impossible. Before reform in Bulgaria, security agreements were filed in some 400 scattered and unlinked notarial registries (see box 3.7).

Modern systems have one national notice filing archive (or separate archives linked by computer or feeding into a central database) or a notice filing archive for each state or province. The law specifies priority based on the time of filing in the archive.

LACK OF ADVANCE FILING AND BLOCKING

Unreformed registries often have no system for advance filings or for reservation of a ranking of priority ("blocking"). That means that between the time a lender checks for prior encumbrances against a potential borrower's collateral and the time it grants the loan, another party could file a more senior security interest against the same collateral. The only remedy is to delay disbursement of the loan to check for other, higher-priority lenders. But for some transactions, like an import for which payment is required before delivery, the lender would not be protected.

Modern notice filing systems permit both advance filing and blocking.

HIGH FEES FOR FILING

Unreformed systems often set high registration fees or impose high costs through prerequisites for registration. Requiring that a registration be notarized, for example, could mean a fee as high as 15 percent of the value of the loan. For 30-day inventory or accounts receivable financing, such a charge would be incurred monthly. Even an apparently modest 1 percent fee, incurred each month to refile the security agreement, would be equivalent to more than 12 percent annually. That could exceed the interest charge on the loan, substantially raising the cost of inventory and accounts receivable financing. The registry itself may charge a high fee—or impose high costs in terms of waiting time for staff or the time to first comply with additional steps, such as providing proof of tax payments or business licenses. Of course, lenders often pay the filing fees, then transfer them to the borrower as part of the loan costs and fees.

Reformed systems are cheap. Charges by North American registries range between $2.50 and $15.00 per registration. These costs are negligible compared with the average loan size in the region. Forms are simple, and the business people entering into security agreements typically fill out the forms themselves, without the aid of a lawyer, and file them from their own offices.

NO INTERNET-BASED SYSTEMS FOR FILING OR INFORMATION RETRIEVAL

Unreformed systems require a physical visit to the registry for filing or information retrieval. These systems either have many branches, at a huge cost to the state—or only a few branches, to which private parties must travel, at a huge cost to the private sector. Often the registries do not have computers. But when they do, the computer systems are desktop or network based. These require a great deal of maintenance and training of operators and are unsuitable for use by the general public.

Modern systems are Internet based. An entire filing system is served by one computer program on a web server. Foreign and domestic lenders—indeed, anyone with Internet access—can search the filing system with a free web browser.[6] Those with the right to file can write to the database by entering a password. Lenders can immediately check the filing for correctness. Once such a system is set up, monthly operating costs can be as low as $200. This cost is negligible relative to the volume of filing. It is also tiny compared with the cost of traditional registries using paper or local network computer systems, and the cost of setting up a government technical office to maintain the registry server's database. Consider the difference in staffing needs. El Salvador's unreformed registry system has more than 1,000 employees. The State of California's Internet-based notice filing archive serves one of the world's 10 largest economies with 10 employees. Romania's filing archive, the world's most advanced when completed in 2000, operates with 1 supervisory official. The first to accept Internet filings, it has more filings than the combined total in a selected group of other reformed archives in Central and Eastern Europe (see figure 6.2 in chapter 6).

UNCOMPETITIVE SUPPLY OF REGISTRY SERVICES

Unreformed registry systems are nearly always operated by the state. Sometimes these state-operated systems provide reasonable service, but mostly they do not. Indeed, operation is typically so poor as to defeat the purpose of the law.

Reformed systems occasionally create publicly operated filing archives that seem to work well. But the best systems bring in the private sector. This has to be done very carefully, however. A monopoly concession to private operators may have satisfactory results, as it has in several Canadian provinces. But a private monopoly coupled with weak government regulation can produce the very worst scenario.

Better systems provide more incentives for good performance. Colombia's registry is operated by the Chamber of Commerce under light supervision by the government—and is equal to some of the best in North America. The Chamber of Commerce operates as a nonprofit organization responding to the broad Colombian business community. The Romanian system relies more on competition. Business associations (including the Chamber of Commerce and the Union of Public Notaries) have formed a nonprofit consortium to operate the filing archive database under the supervision of the Ministry of Justice. By law the consortium can charge filing fees only high enough to cover operational costs (about $200 a month plus the cost of the government supervisor). The consortium licenses members and others to provide filing services. Each provider can charge whatever premium over the core charge it thinks it can justify for the service it gives. Some specialize in cheap, "no frills" filing; others add value with different services. The market decides the winning combinations.

ENFORCEMENT: PROBLEMS THAT PREVENT RAPID SEIZURE AND SALE OF COLLATERAL

The faster and more cheaply property can be seized and sold, the more value it has as collateral. Unreformed systems present many barriers to rapid seizure and sale of collateral—the procedures collectively called *enforcement*—after a borrower defaults on a secured loan.

Slow enforcement poses particular problems for movable property that depreciates rapidly. Fruit, flowers, and fresh fish last only a few days. Accounts receivable are paid in 30–60 days. Dresses and computers lose their value when the new models come out. Even storable agricultural commodities depreciate rapidly without proper care, which is often beyond the ability of a desperate defaulting debtor.

Firms often have a broad mix of movable property. A flour mill and bakery enterprise might have an inventory of bread and rolls lasting only a day, inventories of flour and dry pasta lasting a year, and ovens lasting more than 10 years. Flaws in the enforcement process can make much of this property useless as collateral.

In unreformed systems, where enforcement is carried out by the courts, the process is estimated to take between one and three years—by which time most movable property will have lost all or most of its value.

In unreformed civil code systems enforcement follows a three-stage process under the code of civil procedure. First, the creditor files a complaint and the debtor responds. Depending on the procedure, the debtor may delay by filing defenses (legal reasons for delay). Next, the judge issues a decision in the case and, if in favor of the creditor, issues an order to seize and sell the collateral, after which a court official seizes the property. Finally, the court sells the property under a court-administered process of appraisal and auction or, if the property is occupied, such as in the case of real estate or boats, evicts the occupants, again under a court-administered process. In unreformed common law systems enforcement normally follows the same three stages. For some specifically identified goods taken as collateral, however, some common law jurisdictions permit a bailiff to bypass these three steps.

Lenders operating in unreformed systems report problems at all stages of the process. They describe court-dominated processes with uncertain outcomes, with judges' interpretations of the law differing substantially. All steps of the process are slow and complex. Courts are typically overloaded with cases, with each judge facing a backlog of hundreds of cases and only a few judicial executors licensed to foreclose on collateral.

Court-administered procedures are costly. Often courts levy charges for each court session; sometimes the court filing requires a judicial fee based on the total amount claimed even if that amount is not recovered. Some court procedures require representation by attorneys, who are permitted to collude on their minimum fees. Court-administered sales use expensive appraisal and auction systems, with fees of appraisers and auctioneers set in a quasi-monopolistic way. These costs come out of the proceeds of the collateral and are borne by the creditor and the debtor. Often creditors count themselves lucky to get 20 percent of the value of the collateral, and that only after enduring one to three years of depreciation.

The court procedures mandated by unreformed laws to seize property can involve many delays. They require that a secured lender get a court order for seizure in order to repossess collateral. These laws also offer the debtor many defenses. And they often require serving legal process on the debtor, which can be difficult when a debtor has died or fled the area. Some of the defenses for debtors have a solid public policy basis. But when they are permitted to delay the order for seizure, they carry a high price for borrowers in loss of access to credit.

Another source of delay in the process is the reliance on police—court police or ordinary public police, depending on the system—to enforce the orders for repossession. These police forces are undermanned and undermotivated.

Modern systems permit private repossession of collateral as long as it does not breach the peace. What this means varies with the jurisdiction. Generally it means that creditors cannot use force against the debtor or break into private property. That usually allows a creditor's agents to take motor vehicles from public parking areas or haul away equipment from farms or open construction sites. Sometimes it allows the creditor's agents to enter private property without breaking locks. For example, they could repossess a car if the debtor's garage is left open or the car is parked in an open field or garden. Through a security interest's features of attaching to the collateral no matter who holds it (except often for consumer purchases), floating in a broad category of property, and continuing in proceeds, reformed laws extend that power of private repossession to property of the debtor that may be in the hands of third parties, who must then cooperate in the enforcement process. For example, using the rules for continuation in proceeds, a lender could go to the bank where the debtor had deposited the proceeds of the sale of collateral and use the court order to claim the funds.

When force is required for repossession, modern laws give strict instructions to judges that limit the length of the judicial process for issuing a repossession order. At the creditor's request, if the creditor alleges that payment has not been made and shows proof of its security interest, the judge must issue the order. The debtor need not be present. Modern systems usually give the debtor many more rights than unreformed systems, though not the right to prevent seizure of the collateral if the debtor has not made the scheduled payment on the loan that the collateral secures. Modern systems also levy large penalties against creditors who abuse this process.

Private repossession has its legal roots in the right of parties to contract freely and dispose of their property as they wish. This right permits the law to allow the debtor and the creditor to agree on alternative collection measures if the debtor should default. In keeping with the voluntary nature of such agreements, the law should specifically forbid creditors from using the assistance—or even the presence—of any government official such as the police without a court order.

Modern jurisdictions use the public police where force is required to enforce the court order. In unreformed jurisdictions, where public police may not be able to perform this duty well, it may be necessary to expand the role of private agents (similar to the bailiffs in most common law countries and the Netherlands) or change the incentives for the public police.

COURT-ADMINISTERED SALES

Unreformed laws provide for complex, multi-tiered systems for appraisal and auction of collateral that are administered by the court. The procedures are long and slow, and sometimes other laws and regulations impose other impediments, such as forbidding the sale of collateral for less than the amount of the loan. Ostensibly designed to protect the debtor, the laws fail in that purpose. Fees of the court, attorneys, and auctioneers typically absorb most of the value of the collateral. The result: the lender does not get fully paid, and nothing is left over for the debtor.

Modern systems permit the creditor to sell the collateral as long as it conducts the sale in a commercially reasonable manner, and provide severe penalties for breaching this obligation. These systems thus place the responsibility for sale in the hands of those with the greatest incentive to maximize the value of the collateral and not divert proceeds to other uses. They give detailed instructions about how the creditor shall return to the debtor any balance remaining after the collateral is sold and the loan is paid, and provide heavy penalties for failing to do this.

HOMESTEAD AND EXEMPT PROPERTY PROVISIONS

How the law protects small debtors has great impact in debt collection. Most secured lending laws contain homestead and exempt property provisions protecting debtors from the seizure of certain property. Just as societies have learned that enslaving, imprisoning, dismembering, or killing defaulting debtors is not in the public interest, so they have learned that sending debtors into the world destitute serves no public policy purpose. All countries impose limits on debt colection. No country allows a debtor's bed, shoes, or clothes to be taken, for example.

But most unreformed laws do not balance the need for exemption provisions with the need to provide access to credit. Often such codes state explicitly that no creditor may take from a borrower the tools of the borrower's trade. This apparently well-intentioned provision can cut off credit to small producers. Knowing that the courts will not enforce any contract offering such property as collateral, lenders will not make loans secured by such property. Similarly, where unreformed laws prohibit seizing private residences and farms, banks will not make mortgage loans.

Reformed laws contain more carefully drafted homestead and exempt property provisions, balancing these competing interests in a way that permits a larger flow of credit to the poor.

DELAY CAUSED BY BANKRUPTCY PROCEDURES

Some laws permit the administrator of bankruptcy proceedings to suspend the enforcement of security interests. The public policy merits of such exceptions must be discussed country by country. But whatever their merits, they can incapacitate a secured lending framework—because they mean that lenders cannot count on collateral if borrowers face serious payment difficulties.

Reformed systems limit or eliminate the ability of bankruptcy procedures to delay enforcement of security interests.

NOTES

1. Many legal systems define the nonpossessory pledge (in which the collateral remains in the borrower's possession) in the commercial code, while elsewhere defining small farmers as noncommercial entities—and thus excluding them from using the commercial pledge (as El Salvador's commercial code does, for example). It is unclear whether this common exclusion of farmers from commercial entities is a misguided attempt to protect them or an accidental by-product of attempts to restrict debt collection systems to "better informed" merchants.

2. For example, in most countries the law specifies a minimum amount of property or types of property that creditors cannot seize (see the discussion on homestead exclusion in the enforcement section in this chapter).

3. An important exception, which must be treated carefully in any reformed law, is the loan given by a seller of goods to the buyer. When the seller delivers goods to the buyer and requests payment 30 days later, the seller is making a loan to the buyer. Modern systems give that seller an automatic and unregistered first-priority security interest in those goods. Secured lenders, especially those financing inventory, must carefully investigate the size of this outstanding debt when making a loan. This is the only crucial exception to the first-to-file priority rule, an exception made to permit competition from sellers on credit.

4. In some civil code systems the owner of a fixture acquires an interest in the property to which it is attached.

5. Leasing is considered a security interest under U.S. and Canadian law and a hybrid secured transaction under most civil code regimes because it is a transaction made for purposes of security. In leasing, the creditor retains ownership of the collateral, leasing it to the debtor under various options to purchase.

6. Internet Explorer, Firefox, Netscape, and Opera will all work with most filing archives.

Annex 3.1

FEATURES OF REFORMED AND UNREFORMED SYSTEMS FOR SECURED TRANSACTIONS

CREATION

Feature	Reformed systems	Unreformed systems	Economic effect of unreformed systems
Coverage of goods and transactions	• Allow security interests to be created by any lender and borrower, in any present or future property, and in all transactions.	• Do not cover all types of movable property, lenders, borrowers, and transactions. • May exclude goods that do not yet exist, such as future crops. • May exclude intangible assets. • May exclude fixtures (movable property that has been attached to real estate).	• Goods that have economic importance and value may not be used as collateral under the law, simply because the law will not uphold the security interest. • Vast amounts of "dead capital" result because assets typically owned by firms are useless for accessing credit.
Whether rules on description of collateral permit general (floating) description or require specific identification	• Allow the creditor and debtor to describe the collateral in any way they choose—whether in general terms ("300 head of cattle") or specific ("Hereford bull, tattoo #123"). • Allow the composition of collateral to change. • Permit security interests to float on a broadly defined set of goods serving as inventory, or on accounts receivable or chattel paper.	• Do not allow security agreements to describe the collateral in general terms. • Require security agreements to specifically identify collateral, such as each item of an inventory. • Do not consider pledged inventories (wheat, appliances) as assets with a security interest once they leave the warehouse or change in composition.	• For most economic transactions goods that could serve as collateral are difficult to identify specifically. • Loans can be impossible to monitor because of the need to track each specific item of collateral (such as a specific cow rather than "one cow"). • Inventory cannot serve as collateral. • Accounts receivable and chattel paper cannot serve as collateral.
Whether rules on description of collateral allow use of after-created or after-acquired property	• Permit all property, whether it presently exists or not, to serve as collateral for a loan.	• Permit pledging only of collateral that presently exists ("present collateral"). • May take small steps toward after-acquired collateral by permitting specific pledges such as of a future crop. Cannot cover all possible transformations of goods.	• Lenders cannot finance a farmer before the crop is planted or a manufacturer before the output is created. • Producers cannot obtain financing for inputs secured by future outputs, even though the transformation from inputs to outputs is precisely the point at which producers most need working capital.

(continued on next page)

Annex 3.1 *(continued)*

FEATURES OF REFORMED AND UNREFORMED SYSTEMS FOR SECURED TRANSACTIONS

PRIORITY

Feature	Reformed systems	Unreformed systems	Economic effect of unreformed systems
Establishing priority	• Allow a creditor or seller on credit to establish a ranking among those who might have a claim against property offered as collateral, and make that ranking public. • Do not rely on a possessory system, in which the borrower must physically give the collateral to the creditor while the loan is outstanding (as with pawnshops or warehousing systems). • Use first-to-file basis to determine priority, and designate the place or means for making the security interest public.	• Do not set clear rules for ranking priority among different creditors or different systems for registering security interests. • Often rely only on priority through possession, in which the borrower physically gives the collateral to the creditor. This is especially so in Asian and European civil code systems. • Are unclear about how priority is determined when pledged goods are transferred from a nonpossessory to a possessory system.	• Because lenders cannot determine their position in the ranking of claims against collateral, they cannot determine the value of a good as collateral. • Priority through possession can work for valuables and sometimes for inventory, but not for standing and future crops, equipment, fixtures, and vehicles. • Priority through possession limits the collateral that can be pledged because collateral, once possessed by the lender, becomes worthless to the borrower as a productive input.
Priority rules for future advances	• Set out priority rules for future advances. • For credit lines that are paid down and then drawn on again, extend the same priority to subsequent advances as was assigned to the initial advance.	• Do not set out priority rules for future advances. • For credit lines that are paid down and then drawn on again, do not extend the same priority to subsequent advances as was assigned to the initial advance. Lead to ambiguous status for lenders extending a credit line once it is paid down.	• It is virtually impossible for lenders to safely offer revolving credit lines to borrowers. • Borrowers cannot access credit lines secured by second trusts. • Lending environment is less competitive. Borrowers are essentially tied to one lender, since second or third lenders will be less secure about their priority status.
Continuation in proceeds of a security interest	• Permit a security interest to continue indefinitely in proceeds (as when an inventory is sold for cash), limited only by the ability to trace those proceeds.	• Do not permit a security interest to continue in proceeds, as when an asset, through its sale, is transformed into cash.	• Once a pledged asset is transformed (such as from fertilizer to grain, or from grain to cash), the lender must go to court to get a new security interest in the transformed product.

Annex 3.1 *(continued)*

PRIORITY

Feature	Reformed systems	Unreformed systems	Economic effect of unreformed systems
	• Allow lenders to be confident of retaining their earlier priority and being able to have other private agents assist in collecting debt.	• May permit partial continuation in proceeds—for example, covering the transformation of fertilizer into grain but perhaps not the transformation of grain into cash.	• Every time the lender goes to court, the lender faces risk of delay, risk of loss of priority to another lender, and additional costs. • The transaction costs and risks for lenders increase substantially.
Limits for fixtures	• Separate the framework for securing loans with movable property and fixtures from the framework for mortgaging the principal real estate.	• Treat fixtures as movable property until they are affixed to real estate, when they become subject to the legal regime governing real estate. • Consider pledged equipment, once attached to real estate, as subject to any mortgage against that real estate, so that the creditor loses priority status to the lenders holding the mortgage.	• No lender will finance the purchase or sale on credit of fixtures without also having a first trust on the real estate to which the fixtures are attached. • No loans are likely to be made for furnaces, generators, and the like.
Rules for ranking priority of tax claims and liens by the state	• Assign priority to tax claims, liens, and state debts on the basis of the time of filing a notice in the public filing archive.	• Do not set out clear rules for ranking the priority of a security interest relative to tax claims. • May create conflict between secured claims of private creditors and priority given by law for state tax liens. • Where state's claims are not public, make it impossible for potential lenders to tell in advance whether tax liens exist against collateral.	• The ability of the state to place its claims before those of private creditors, regardless of when or whether it filed the claims, fatally undercuts the secured lending system. • Laws contradicting one another compound lenders' uncertainty and thus lower the value of property as collateral.
Unified or multiple systems of establishing priority?	• Apply one system of priorities to all security interests as well as to all other transactions undertaken for security, including leases and conditional sales.	• Do not have a comprehensive priority system for all secured transactions. For example, leasing law might require registration in a different system than the one in which pledges are registered.	• Potential lenders that wish to take property as collateral need to check more than one system to learn of other encumbrances against the collateral.

(continued on next page)

Annex 3.1 *(continued)*

FEATURES OF REFORMED AND UNREFORMED SYSTEMS FOR SECURED TRANSACTIONS

PUBLICITY

Feature	Reformed systems	Unreformed systems	Economic effect of unreformed systems
Cost, accessibility, and quality of registry	• Publicize security interests through a notice filing system that allows any potential lender to quickly determine whether collateral offered by a borrower has a prior security interest. Provide an Internet-based system for movable property collateral, allowing national and international access to notices of security interests. • Maintain filing archives that are user friendly, low cost, and quick. Typical cost in North America is between $2.50 and $15.00 per registration. • Require the filing of only minimal information about a security interest (name, description, date of filing). • Permit but do not require the use of state and notary certifications.	• Require permission of authorities to access registry, and do not allow public access. May leave it up to judges to determine who can have access. • May have a registry that is not computerized. Registration systems may rely on antiquated filing methods, such as public announcements or newspaper advertisements. • May have a fragmented registry system, with multiple and unlinked registries in different jurisdictions. • Charge high fees for registration. Notary fees to process filings can range between 2 percent and 15 percent of loan value. Fees are charged monthly for inventory or accounts receivable financing.	• Where lenders do not have access to the registry system, they cannot verify their priority status. • Where there are multiple registries, lenders will not know which to search to discover what property a business has pledged. • Where registries are based on courts or notaries, determining priority can be impossible. • Filing becomes too cumbersome and costly relative to the value of loans, for both borrowers and creditors.
Advance filing and blocking	• Permit advance filings and reservation of a ranking of priority ("blocking").	• May have no system for advance filings or for reservation of a ranking of priority.	• Between the time a lender checks for prior encumbrances against a potential borrower's collateral and the time it grants the loan, another party could file a more senior security interest against the same collateral.
Supply of registry services—public or private?	• Can authorize private companies to operate a central database, with supervisory and regulatory powers established by law. Requiring universal technical standards and nonproprietary software and hardware for the database can support competition.	• Have a registry that is run by the state or by a private monopoly as a state concession.	• Monopoly supply usually means high prices and poor service.

Annex 3.1 *(continued)*

ENFORCEMENT

Feature	Reformed systems	Unreformed systems	Economic effect of unreformed systems
Time frame for enforcing procedures	• Allow harmless repossession and creditor-administered sale of collateral. Through civil procedure law, provide for ex parte court orders (orders that can be issued even if the debtor is not present) to use force when necessary.	• In civil code systems, require a three-stage process for enforcement: the lender requests an order to execute from the court, a court official seizes the property, and the property is sold under a court-administered process of appraisal and auction. (In some common law systems a bailiff may reduce these steps.) • Involve costly court-administered procedures, with courts sometimes levying charges for each session.	• Systems result in court-dominated processes with uncertain outcomes, with judges interpreting the same laws in different ways. • Estimated time for execution ranges between one and three years, due to extreme backlogs of court cases.
Seizure of collateral	• Allow only proof that debt payment has been made as defense against seizure. • Have some homestead or exempt property provisions protecting against the seizure of certain property, but these strike a good balance between protecting the vulnerable and protecting the rights of creditors.	• Require that secured party have a court order for seizure. • Permit many challenges to the legal process, each of which can delay the order for seizure. • With a court order for seizure, require that court police seize property—but there are often few such officials and a low priority on rapid execution. • Strike a poor balance in homestead and exempt property provisions, with excessive protection of debtors (such as in preventing seizure of tools of a borrower's trade).	• Exempting equipment from seizure can cut off credit to small producers. Knowing that courts will not enforce the seizure of equipment, lenders will not accept it as collateral.
Sale of collateral	• Give parties freedom to agree on terms of sale for collateral. • Require creditors to notify debtors and junior secured creditors before sale of collateral. • Allow creditors to retain collateral in complete satisfaction of secured debt (strict foreclosure).	• Rely on complex, court-administered systems of appraisal and auction of collateral. • May forbid sale of collateral for less than amount of loan.	• Where enforcement (seizure and sale) takes one to three years, it makes most classes of movable property (accounts receivable, perishable goods) useless as collateral, because they do not maintain their economic value that long. • With costly court-administered sales, lenders do not get paid and nothing is left over for debtors.

CHAPTER 4

DETERMINING THE CONTENT OF THE REFORM

Expanding the use of collateral requires reforming the law of secured transactions and, as a critical part of that reform, replacing the traditional registry with an archive for filing notices of security interests.[1] The reform must tackle a wide array of commercial and microeconomic problems, many examples of which are discussed in chapter 3. The law, through its detail, must address each of the commercial problems inexpensively and effectively. It must give clear instructions that address a daunting set of microeconomic problems. And through all this, the law must constantly guide economic agents toward actions that produce the greatest economic gain at the lowest cost.

Moreover, the detail must be integrated into the new law's architecture in a way that produces the best overall impact. And this architecture must fit within the framework of other laws in a way that permits the new law of secured transactions to operate in an economically effective way.

COVERING THE DETAIL

As chapter 3 shows, unreformed laws prevent important classes of property from serving as collateral, block the use of collateral in certain transactions, and prevent some agents from offering collateral and others from accepting it. A reformed law will need to cover many more situations than those discussed in that chapter. Indeed, a well-drafted law will cover all the detail of a modern textbook on secured transactions, which typically contains several hundred pages.[2] In setting out that detail, the law must resolve some larger strategic issues that arise in drafting the law and transforming the registry into a filing archive. These issues are set out in the following sections.

SHAPING THE ARCHITECTURE

The law, at its most detailed level, is like a computer program that must permit lenders and borrowers to process an enormous range of economic transactions.

But that detail operates within an overall structure, the architecture of the law, that also affects its economic impact. The legal issues that must be addressed in shaping this architecture will arise again and again, so the project team and task manager should have a clearly developed and defensible position on the law's approach to solving problems in creation, priority, publicity, and enforcement and in the derogation (amendment or repeal) of conflicting laws.

CREATION

Two fundamental issues that the reform must address: Will the law adopt a unified approach covering all transactions that function as security devices? And how will it apply to nonconsensual security interests?

Comprehensive functional approach

The secured transactions reform that is most economically effective, the North American model, adopts the comprehensive functional approach, with the reformed law covering all voluntary security devices that use property. These include mainly pledges, leases, trusts, conditional sales, consignments, warehouse finance, and mortgages against ships and airplanes.[3]

That means that if a transaction, no matter what it is called, takes property as collateral, the reformed law will determine priority and publicity. If in addition the transaction takes collateral on a voluntary basis, the reformed law will also determine creation and enforcement. It does not mean that the new law repeals all the old laws specifying security devices. Those voluntary security devices will continue to exist. But the reform will impose uniformity in key aspects over all these devices: priority will be determined by the time of filing in the filing archive, and repossession and sale will be governed by the new law. That will require minor modifications of the other laws. But as long as the filing archive is inexpensive (as it should be for many other reasons), the modifications relating to priority should not inconvenience those using the existing legal features. And the new provisions relating to enforcement will typically be an advantage.

An alternative strategy, the superpledge-supercharge approach, calls for strengthening the traditional legal instrument for the many types of security interests in movable property that may now exist. Depending on the regime, this would relate to the pledge, the charge, and the mortgage. This is the approach suggested in the European Bank for Reconstruction and Development's draft model law on secured transactions (see the appendix).

The problem with this strategy is that it leaves the new law separate from those governing other security devices, such as conditional sales. Logically, this fragmented approach is inferior to the comprehensive functional approach because it increases the chance of conflicts in priority—and the greater the chance of conflicts, the greater the risk to the lender of losing the collateral and thus the lower the value of property as collateral. In the United States confusion over priority arising from the growing number of security devices was among the factors that led to the creation of the comprehensive functional approach in the mid-20th century, as part of the first legal reform ever undertaken (embodied in Article 9 of the U.S. Uniform Commercial Code). Countries like Mexico and Peru, which have modeled their laws on specific laws in industrial countries yet have not introduced the umbrella of the comprehensive functional approach, have had poor records in the use of movable property as collateral.[4]

The lack of a body of evaluations of secured transactions reform projects rules out a definitive judgment on the relative merits of these two approaches. Still, there are some partial indications. A recent survey by the EBRD ranked the reforms in Romania—which followed the North American model of a comprehensive functional approach—as the best among a selected group of reformers in Central and Eastern Europe (see figure 6.2 in chapter 6). The reforms judged to be less successful used a mix of models, some comprehensive and some based on the superpledge-supercharge approach. In developing countries undergoing reform there is typically little political opposition to the comprehensive functional approach. Instead, it is in industrial countries of Europe that opposition to this approach seems to arise (apparently largely because much of the legal community and the banking system sees little need to change). Where opposition does exist, the superpledge-supercharge approach may be most feasible.

Full application only for consensual security interests

The reformed law of secured transactions should have limited application to nonconsensual security interests—private liens and judgments, including judgments arising in collecting unsecured loans, government tax liens, and child support payments. While the law should include them in its provisions on priority and publicity, it should exclude them from its provisions on creation (because they are not voluntary) and from enforcement (because they require court enforcement).

Any reform project not observing this distinction between voluntary security interests (where the borrower agrees to use property as collateral before signing the loan) and involuntary security interests (where the borrower has not agreed to do so) will face insurmountable political opposition to any measure to simplify the process for seizing and selling property. Enforcing security interests, whether consensual or nonconsensual, requires taking something away from someone to satisfy a claim. Sometimes enforcement takes place over the objection of the person with the interest in the underlying property. Any well-functioning system of property rights closely guards the process by which a person's property can be taken without that person's consent. This is an important economic feature of a property rights system: without property rights over inputs and outputs, the incentive systems for private agents would collapse.

In the debate over the law, exactly how property serving as collateral will be transferred to the lender will therefore be a hotly contested issue. It requires integrating two potentially conflicting principles typically embodied in national constitutions: the right of people to enjoy due process of law when their property is being taken, and their right to freely dispose of their property. The key to integrating these two principles lies in the borrower's voluntary decision to offer collateral: the right to freely dispose of one's property includes the right to offer it as collateral for a loan and permit the lender to take the collateral without court intervention. The consensual nature of offering collateral—no one forces the borrower to do so—is central to reconciling the draft law with the constitutional provisions on due process.

For this reason the law of secured transactions must fully apply only to consensual transactions—and should not govern the creation of involuntary security interests or the collection of the underlying property. For these nonvoluntary seizures of property the debtor can claim full legal process. That is crucial in leaving undisturbed the rights of the state and other parties to create involuntary claims in accordance with other laws and for those subject to those claims to dispute them in court.

Full separation of the voluntary and involuntary systems, however, could create havoc in the system for secured transactions: if involuntary judgments have priority over voluntary claims on collateral, claims on collateral will have full value only if a borrower will never be subject to involuntary claims. That is impossible for either the lender or the borrower to know. So the reform must merge the two systems when it comes to the priority and publicity of nonconsensual claims, ensuring that the priority of these claims is based on the time of filing in a security interest filing archive.

PRIORITY

To have the maximum economic effect, the new law must determine the priority of security interests by the time at which the notice of their existence is filed in the archive. Using "date of creation" or some other standard creates problems in determining priority. In addition, the law must ensure that the priority system precludes hidden liens. And as discussed, it should extend the priority system to nonconsensual claims, particularly to government claims under taxes and debt collection.

PUBLICITY

For the reasons noted in chapter 3, best practice for publicizing security interests relies on an archive for filing notices, not on a registry.[5] Filing a notice of the existence of a security agreement eliminates the needless and costly steps of state verification of the security agreement and filing of original copies. It also permits the filing archive to be a simple, inexpensive Internet-based database. Modern standards call for Internet-based filing and search, using web-based software. Dial-up access is a distant second best, because it requires installing programs on each desktop computer that accesses the archive. Under no circumstances should the archive be paper based.

The role of public and private entities in the administration of the archive is an important judgment call for the project team and the country. Many administrative systems—public, private, and mixed—are in use. As noted in chapter 3, Romania's archive is operated by a consortium of nongovernmental organizations under the supervision of a small government unit, much as Colombia's commercial registry system is. As also noted, this archive was ranked the best performer among a selected group of reformers in Central and Eastern Europe (see figure 6.2 in chapter 6). Bulgaria's, another good performer, apparently operates under a government agency. Government-operated registries can work, but they always involve risks. They often divert registry revenues to other purposes and use up registry budgets in hiring political appointees rather than maintaining equipment.

The reform should avoid the common error of institution building aimed at modernizing a registry without modernizing the law that governs it. This is a fruitless enterprise. Transforming the registry into a filing archive is not a stand-alone reform involving merely computers and training. It must instead be part of the legal reform, since both the registry and its successor filing archive must do what the law specifies.

ENFORCEMENT

Speeding up enforcement is an essential part of the reform, to ensure that rapidly depreciating movable property will have value as collateral. All successful reforms have limited the scope for judicial intervention at the enforcement stage. Indeed, best practice minimizes the role of judges and gives maximum support to private repossession and privately administered sale. The reformed law should limit judicial discretion in issuing orders for repossession to considering only whether the debtor paid, and instruct the judge to make that decision even in an ex parte process, where the debtor is not present. A key to success is the law's mode for creating security interests, which should build a web of private incentives that support the creditor in seeking enforcement of the claim against collateral.

Departures from this best practice model for enforcement need to be carefully evaluated by an economist and an international legal expert to determine their impact on the economic effect of the reform.

DEROGATING CONFLICTING LAWS

The new law will contradict other laws, and the contradictory passages of these laws must be amended or repealed—or derogated. The more inconsistencies the new law resolves, the lower the chance that settling a transaction will require a lawsuit. That is, the greater the consistency, the lower the risk and the transaction costs involved in lending. The reformed law should include a section identifying the laws being derogated, with commentaries to allay concerns that lawyers and policymakers will have about upsetting existing arrangements and creating unforeseen problems.

Derogations of laws with public policy objectives need careful attention. One such case involved Bolivia's mining law of the mid-1950s, which, in a passage aimed at strengthening miners' property rights, stated that no one could take a miner's tools. Derogation of that section required a detailed explanation of why this derogation would not lead to lending secured by a miner's tools. Another case was Ukraine's family law, which, in prohibiting the eviction of any family with a child under age 12, made lending secured by housing very risky. The reformed law on secured transactions referenced discussions of alternative protections for families with minors, though these protections were not implemented.

Some lazily drafted reform laws simply declare that the new law derogates all conflicting provisions of any other law. This approach cuts costs by eliminating the legal research needed to identify points of conflict. But it also makes every loan an invitation to a lawsuit, since all conflicts between a lender and a borrower must be decided anew by a court. When two laws disagree and each claims to derogate conflicting provisions in other laws, the logical outcome is indeterminate—a situation that mainly generates fees for litigators.

NOTES

1. Of course, a government could, without reforming the law, set up a lender that takes collateral and offers better rates for secured than for unsecured loans. But by making loans refused by the private sector, the government lending program would be assuming the risks and bearing the losses that the private sector seeks to avoid— and would continuously accumulate losses. Such a program thus offers no viable solution to the problem of inadequate support for collateral.

2. Drafting such a law will require the assistance of legal experts skilled in writing laws of secured transactions. This task is beyond the skill set of nonlawyers as well as many lawyers without special training in secured transactions law. For a discussion of these staffing requirements, see chapter 5.

3. As a purely legal point, no system includes all security devices. For example, a wholesaler selling goods on credit to a merchant has a first-priority claim against those goods even if no security interest is filed in the archive. Similar exemptions apply to small consignments (for example, by artisans) to retailers. In addition, some regimes place the security interest system for ships and planes outside the general framework and apply special laws to them. (These systems predate modern reforms but are often subject to international agreements, so that the transaction costs of changing them are high.) These are finer points that the law must cover. None of them changes the fundamental fact that the more transactions covered and the lower the cost of covering them, the greater the economic gains from reform will generally be.

4. The World Bank Group's Doing Business indicators rank Mexico and Peru in the bottom decile in the world on the efficacy of secured transactions laws. See http://www.doingbusiness.org/ExploreTopics/GettingCredit/.

5. Other useful references on filing archives include European Bank for Reconstruction and Development, *Publicity of Security Rights: Guiding Principles for the Development of a Charges Registry* (London, 2004; http://www.ebrd.com/country/sector/law/st/core/pubsec.pdf); Daniel Bénay, Ronald C. C. Cuming, and Catherine Walsh, *Law and Policy Reform at the Asian Development Bank: A Guide to Movables Registries* (Manila: Asian Development Bank, 2002); and E. T. Wohlers, "The Registry: Essential Element in Secured Lending," *Arizona Journal of International and Comparative Law* 18 (2001): 711–19.

CHAPTER 5

IMPLEMENTING THE REFORM

A successful reform of the law of secured transactions requires a modern law and a modern filing archive. The law must be passed, and the filing archive implemented. How does a task manager achieve this?

Among the most important tasks is to build a persuasive case for the reform. The more persuasive that case is, the stronger the position of the donor or international financial institution in the country dialogue will be and the easier it will be to get agreement on the reform. The key to reaching a voluntary agreement on reform with the government is a law and filing system that seem reasonable to the interested parties. Both the economic and the political approach of the reform must therefore be well justified.

A good place to set out the detailed case for reform is the diagnostic study. Its analysis can be reinforced by commentaries in the draft law giving the motivation, legal background, and economic logic underlying the drafting strategy. The full package—the diagnostic study, draft law, and proposed filing archive—will need to be defended in a training and public awareness program that addresses people's concerns, well founded and otherwise. Putting this package together will require a team of lawyers and economists, including both local and international experts.

So task managers face challenges on several fronts. They must understand the legal issues well enough to make informed judgments about the quality of the diagnostic study and the legal changes being proposed by an international expert in secured transactions law. They must supervise the interaction between the lawyers and the economists on the team or supervise the firm that supplies the lawyers and economists. They must be prepared to explain and defend the reform, throughout project preparation and later, to key stakeholders in the country—often in the absence of the experts on their team. And they must supervise the foreign and local teams that will assist in this explanation and defense.

CARRYING OUT THE DIAGNOSTIC STUDY

A good reform begins with a good diagnostic study. A good study identifies legal barriers to using collateral. It also distinguishes problems in access to credit attributable to laws from those with other causes—and links those legal problems to their legal roots.

Some diagnostic studies simply list the legal problems in current law. That approach limits their effectiveness. A study that merely identifies a legal constraint—without explaining its economic importance—will be less convincing to key stakeholders. Diagnostic studies need to carefully walk stakeholders through the economic problems arising from the present legal framework, explain the potential economic impact of reform, and show that a solution is feasible within the country's legal and institutional framework. They also need to address public policy problems that arise in derogating (amending or repealing) contradictory laws.

Diagnostic studies are aimed at two broad audiences—legal readers and nonlegal readers. Nonlegal readers—economists, most donor staff, many local officials, local banks and businesses—are accustomed to thinking about constraints on access to credit that stem from economic causes. A good diagnostic study must convince these readers of the economic importance of the legal constraints.

Nonlegal readers may not immediately understand the potential economic impact of relatively obscure legal provisions. Should the law require a precise description of the goods taken as collateral? Should the law permit the borrower to sell the collateral? Should the law provide for the automatic continuation of the security interest in the proceeds of the sale or other disposition of the collateral? Should government tax claims have superpriority? To keep nonlegal readers engaged, the diagnostic study should explain as early as possible why technical details such as these can have an enormous impact on the effectiveness of the secured transactions system and thus on access to credit.

Legal readers—local practicing lawyers and government officials trained as lawyers—have somewhat different needs. Stakeholders trained in the local law will typically have a general understanding of the importance of a framework for secured lending. But they also will often believe that their country already has such a framework. The diagnostic study must therefore convince these readers that the legal problems in access to credit are not just simple differences in approach but differences with great economic importance. Discussing the potential economic gain from reform is important because changing established laws and legal practices always incurs costs. Legal readers, often more sensitive to such costs than other stakeholders, will be more willing to accept that their country should pay those costs if they expect a large economic gain.

The question of economic gain from different legal alternatives weighs heavily on judicial decisions and can influence judicial rulings on constitutionality. So it can be helpful for legal readers if a diagnostic study explains the economic merits of different drafting solutions, giving estimates of the potential gains from different approaches. For example, "this approach will exclude accounts receivable, which represent about 10 percent of business assets."

A good diagnostic study has four key inputs:

- An initial legal assessment based on a preliminary examination of local law that gives the field team some guidance about what to look for in the field interviews.
- Field interviews that investigate the effect of current law on access to credit by sector, including information on the terms of loans and the role of collateral in determining those terms.
- A legal analysis that elaborates on the initial legal assessment, building the microeconomic chain of causation from legal defect to observed characteristic of the credit market. This analysis, following the field interviews, should cite all relevant laws, points of conflict, and internal inconsistencies and identify the economic impact of each shortcoming. Local lawyers, identified by referral or through the field interviews, should be brought fully into this process.
- An economic analysis of the likely impact of reform. This should link the legal defects to what is observed in the credit market, assess the role of alternative explanations, and provide some rough guidance on the likely economic impact of the reform.

INITIAL LEGAL ASSESSMENT

The first step in the diagnostic study, an initial legal assessment of the existing laws governing secured transactions, will point to the questions that the field team should ask in the field interviews. This assessment requires help from both a local secured transactions lawyer and a foreign lawyer with expertise in secured transactions law (typically about 5–10 staff days from each). In addition, indicators relating to secured transactions from the World Bank Group's

Doing Business project can provide a good initial survey of problems (see the discussion of this data source in chapter 6).

The local lawyer should identify the fundamental secured transactions laws and related laws that affect their operation. These laws typically include the bankruptcy law, the homestead and exempt property provisions, the code of civil procedure, the banking laws, and consumer protection laws. But the local lawyer should have enough expertise in the debt collection process to identify any additional laws that are relevant. A good example is the family law in Ukraine that prohibited eviction of any family with a child under the age of 12. This law, clearly a significant constraint on using real estate as collateral, would not rank high on the list of laws that foreign experts would check. Good local lawyers will flag such issues. The local lawyer should also report the local view on the main problems in the debt collection system and options for reform.

The local lawyer will rarely be able to identify all the problems in the underlying laws, however, because the local lawyer will typically have had no training in foreign legal systems that allow effective use of movable property as collateral. Once the local lawyer has found the laws and competent translations and submitted the local view on the source of problems, the diagnostic task therefore passes to the foreign lawyer.

The foreign lawyer needs to check the law for important potential problems in each stage of the secured transactions process—creation, priority, publicity, and enforcement of a security interest. This initial assessment should cover all the material discussed in chapter 3 of this book. But a skilled foreign expert will identify many more problems than are set out in that chapter and should report on whatever else looks important based on a reading of the law. (This book sets out only some of the important problems; most textbooks on secured transactions run 300–500 pages in length.) And of course all these problems must be covered in the proposed law.

The initial legal assessment should produce a list of specific legal problems and their likely economic consequences. An example of the desired specificity: "The pledge law gives priority to the first lender secured by the crop in the field, but the warehouse law gives priority to the warehouseman. Therefore, we would expect to see no loans secured by crops in the field because of the risk of loss of priority arising from transfers of harvested crops to the warehouse." Here the secured finance law sets the fundamental framework for allowing farmers to pledge crops as collateral, but the inconsistency with the warehouse law makes crops economically useless as collateral.

The assessment should be sufficiently specific and understandable to enable someone who is not a lawyer specializing in secured transactions to follow up with questions in the field. Detailed legal citations are not necessary in the initial legal assessment, but clarity for the field mission is.

FIELD INTERVIEWS

Armed with the initial legal assessment, a team should undertake a mission of 5–10 staff days to interview private firms, including banks, nonbank lenders, and borrowers, and the lawyers who represent them. These interviews will test the hypotheses set out in the initial legal assessment and supply the material for the study's discussion of the effect of the law by sector. A team that includes both a lawyer and an economist is desirable. But a team with only economists is acceptable as long as they are well versed in how secured transactions affect business operations.

The field interviews should be aimed primarily at understanding the broader context in which secured transactions take place—whether and how much actual practice corresponds with the law—and secondarily at collecting data. The most important data are those required for the economic analysis—the terms of loans (interest rates, maturities, credit limits, collateral requirements), which should be collected from all lenders and confirmed with borrowers when possible.

While the team should collect data from lenders, it should spend most of its time with such companies as equipment dealers, construction companies, food processing firms, wholesale and retail distributors, and transport companies (freight haulers, bus and taxi companies). These businesses—borrowers and sellers on credit—can make a lot of money by overcoming borrowing constraints, so they can give a clear account of what works and what doesn't. (Banks are often more indifferent about relieving borrowers' constraints, especially where supervision is weak and related-party lending strong.) The order of interviews is not particularly important. Indeed, mixing up the order can provide a good cross-check by enabling the team to ask, say, a bank to comment on the views and information given by, say, an equipment dealer.

Private firms generally give more accurate information on secured transactions than do state-owned firms. The reason is that the government often explicitly or implicitly guarantees the debt of state-owned firms. Consequently, private banks will sometimes accept pledges of movable property from a state-owned firm in the belief that the state will pay the debt if the firm defaults. With a possible state guarantee, a pledge by such a firm gives little information about whether the collateral can actually be repossessed and sold.

The team should handle interviews with local law firms carefully, as local lawyers often know little about the legal framework for debt collection. The team also should watch for skilled practitioners who seem to understand the basic issues, lawyers who could be recruited to aid in drafting the law.

Finally, the team should visit and examine the registry for security interests. This visit can produce important information on how the registry operates and whether the law of secured transactions is actually being used.

Banks and nonbank financial institutions

The team must always interview banks, since they are the main providers of credit to the registered (formal) business sector. But it should also interview leasing companies and microfinance institutions.

BANKS. When interviewing banks, the team should meet with the heads of the credit and legal departments at the same time if possible. Getting the two together in the same room can produce a more complete picture. Credit officers want to lend, and they know what loans are actually being made. Meanwhile, legal departments, often in the position of restraining credit officers, may lack complete information about what credit officers are doing. Bank lawyers also have experience in debt collection, and the team should ask about that experience in detail. If the team is told that certain loans are not made because of bank policy, it should try to see the person who makes that policy.

Interview questions need to be structured carefully to get to the truth of an issue. Take the issue of access to unsecured loans. Banks always have recourse to the real estate of a defaulting borrower: their legal departments have well-established methods of filing liens against that real estate (nonconsensual debt collection). This implicit recourse to real estate in the event of default is a major reason why banks offer unsecured loans to the wealthy (who own property) but not to the poor (who do not). Moreover, when a bank takes a security interest in movable property, it may ultimately be relying on the borrower's real estate holdings for security. So when banks say they offer loans without collateral (which they will often call "guarantees"), the team should ask more questions: Do the banks restrict such loans to people who own real estate? Do they require a cosigner? If they do, who qualifies? Must it be a property owner? The borrower's job supervisor?

Banks will often assert that collateral makes no difference in their lending decisions, claiming that they look only at cash flow, business plans, and payment records. That is generally nonsense. Rather than arguing, however, the team should try to get the terms of unsecured loans, loans for new cars, and loans secured by real estate. Since banks set targets for debt service as a fraction of income or cash flow at about the same level for each type of loan, determining whether banks offer larger loans when borrowers offer collateral is a simple matter of arithmetic.

The team should press hard for the details of automobile finance. Why are interest rates for used cars so much higher than for new ones? Why can the same borrower get a loan for a car but not for an earthmover or a drill press?

Banks can typically give a good account of how the legal framework for real estate operates. Since they have collection departments, they can, more readily than most nonbank lenders and sellers on credit, start proceedings to attach the real estate holdings of a defaulting borrower. To gain a good understanding of the legal and practical limits on using movable property as collateral, however, the team should cross-check the responses of banks with those of dealers and borrowers. For example, if banks say they will lease any kind of equipment, the team should ask firms about their experience in financing equipment with leasing, then discuss their responses with the banks that are interviewed.

LEASING COMPANIES. Interviews of leasing companies should focus on how they repossess leasehold collateral. Is a court procedure necessary or not? And if required, does the lessor ignore the requirement out of a belief that it will not be prosecuted for repossessing leasehold goods without a court order?

The team should be sure to understand the differences in procedures for registered automobiles, other motor vehicles, and other nonregistered property. Because registered automobiles circulate on the public streets, the lessor can readily repossess them if courts permit that. Other property can be harder to repossess. Trucks and buses may cross international borders in the natural course of business. Other leasehold property is not located in public areas. Leasing companies' experience with that property will give much insight into existing practices. In Bangladesh and Uruguay lessors remarked, "We sign the lease. Then we pray."

As an interview progresses, the team should ask, in the most natural and unthreatening way possible, how the leasing company finances itself. The best way is to inquire whether the leases can serve as collateral for loans. Most companies are sensitive about discussing their sources of financing, for many different reasons, some of which are best not to know. An important question is whether the leasing company is owned by a bank. In most lax systems of supervision and regulation, ownership by a bank will give a leasing company nearly automatic access to loans financed by deposits.

MICROFINANCE INSTITUTIONS. The team should ask microfinance institutions how they collect their unsecured loans, raising this issue in the most nonconfrontational way possible, then find out later whether those methods are legal. If the team already knows that a method is illegal, it should ask whether the microfinance institution is concerned about the illegality.

The team should also find out whether microfinance lenders take collateral in any formal way (lease, registered pledge, registered mortgage). Many microlenders, like banks, offer secured as well as unsecured loans.

Finally, the team should ask these lenders for their rate of nonperforming loans and find out whether their portfolio of these loans can serve as collateral with licensed banks or on the capital market.

Sellers on credit

MOTOR VEHICLE DEALERS. Cars are the "gold standard" of movable property as collateral, with trucks and buses close behind. The underlying property is valuable, standard in design, and easy to resell. Even obsolete legal frameworks for secured lending permit repossession and sale of a motor vehicle. And if the lender or seller on credit uses any title retention device (financial lease, sale with retention of title), the car can be privately repossessed whenever the secured party finds it.

So if cars cannot be sold on credit, it is doubtful whether any other movable property can serve as collateral. For this reason interviews with motor vehicle dealers can shed much light on the ability to take movable property as collateral.

When interviewing dealers, the team should ask whether they sell on credit themselves, originate credit-sale contracts that are taken over by a finance company, or rely on banks and finance companies. What are the terms of the loans? Does the dealer or the bank require an additional security interest against real estate or the cosignature of someone who owns real estate—or require that the car purchaser own real estate in order to qualify for financing? In these cases lenders may not be relying on the automobile for collateral, even though they take a security interest in it. They may instead be relying on the ability to attach real estate if the borrower defaults.

Interviewers should ask dealers about both their own credit granting practices and those of banks. Do they believe that banks are financing most borrowers that the dealers consider good borrowers? If not, why not? Because dealers have an enormous profit incentive to understand exactly how to get credit to finance sales, interviewers should also ask dealers why they do not finance such sales out of company resources and then refinance with a bank. The dealers' responses should be cross-checked with banks.

The team should carefully examine sale terms for cars, trucks, and buses to determine whether an alternative collection system exists. In Ukraine, for example, the secured transactions law was unworkable, but cars were nonetheless freely sold on credit because the automobile registration system permitted dual registration. The dealer retained one registration and set of keys while the "owner" had another. If the owner defaulted, the dealer picked up the car. The statements of car dealers and banks should be confirmed with cab drivers and local citizens.

If motor vehicle dealers sell other kinds of equipment, the team should find out whether they will sell a car on credit to a buyer but not another piece of equipment (as dealers often do). If so, why do the dealers treat this equipment differently as collateral?

EQUIPMENT DEALERS. Equipment dealers provide an important cross-check on the views of banks about collateral. These dealers rarely have the staff to maintain extensive collection systems for seizing real estate. Nor do they have the information advantage of banks, which can inspect borrowers' bank accounts and loan portfolios directly. Dealers therefore depend much more on the ability to repossess equipment and can often give a more accurate account of the legal framework for movable collateral.

The team should use the findings from interviews of equipment dealers and wholesalers in its interviews with private banks and organizations of borrowers and of lenders. It should cross-confirm constantly, asking the banks for comments on what the equipment dealers say and, where there are substantial disagreements, asking for a follow-up interview. For example, if Dealer A says that banks always wants the borrower to own real estate and Bank B says that it never asks for real estate, the team should ask Bank B to recommend a dealer that could discuss these policies more along the lines of the bank's account.

An important constraint on any dealer's ability to sell on credit is its own access to credit. So the interviews should determine whether dealers can use credit-sale contracts or inventories of equipment or parts as collateral to expand their access to working capital and to refinance their credit sales. Can new equipment serve as collateral, and if so, is credit advanced to the dealer by the manufacturer or by a bank? Can the dealer use its stock of used machines as collateral, or only new machines? Many dealers get equipment on consignment from manufacturers that are in effect financing the dealers' inventory of new equipment.

Phrasing these questions requires care, because banks sometimes give the appearance of taking all types of collateral, even filing pledges that have no legal foundation. In fact, they may be relying only on the borrowing firm's real estate, maintaining a credit limit equal to a fraction of the firm's real estate holdings no matter how large its holdings of movable property are.

Local lawyers and law firms

Local lawyers who work with banks and sellers on credit can often give valuable perspectives on the debt collection process. But many local lawyers, even at large, reputable firms, have little practical information about the use of movable property or small real estate holdings as collateral because they have no experience in creating or collecting loans secured by such assets. So it is always best to start with the lawyers representing equipment dealers or the collection departments of private banks.

The collection departments of state banks can also be helpful. State banks often have incentive problems, and their collection efforts can sometimes seem ineffective. But these banks are often the only ones that have made loans secured by movable property and that have ever attempted to collect them.

The registry

The team should go to the registry to find out how it operates. What type of computer equipment, operating system, and database system does it use? (If the field mission has an information technology expert, that expert should go along on the visit.) How is the registry administered? In particular, how is it funded, and who gets the proceeds from filing? That information will be important in designing a reform, because registries that stand to lose revenues can often be strong opponents of reform.

The team should see what data the registry collects. If the registry will not give the team data, that is an important commentary on public access to information. If it cannot give the team data, that is an important commentary on the quality of the system.

If data are available, the team should review them and question any anomalies. For example, the Ukrainian registry seemed to be operating well, was technically well designed, and had a large and steadily growing number of filings. But further inquiry found that the filings consisted entirely of tax liens and car loans. The tax liens were filed because the law compelled the government to do so. The filed notices of "pledges" for car loans were just a cover for a parallel automobile registration system using retention of title for the sale of cars on credit.

If the data show that no security interests are being filed, the system is not being used, no matter what the team is told about possibilities and practices under the law.

The team should ask precise questions about public access: Are there any restrictions on who can look, and when? Can people conduct searches themselves, or must they have a registry employee do so? Is there remote public access? If so, how does it work? Is Internet access available or contemplated?

DATA

In the end the most compelling microeconomic case for reform will arise from the initial legal assessment and the field interviews. These will trace causal chains from the law to lending and borrowing behavior with examples that will be familiar to the audience for the diagnostic study. The study should detail the effects of the law by sector (box 5.1).

BOX 5.1

Structuring the diagnostic study

The organization of the diagnostic study is not engraved in stone. But here's one structure that has been successful:

- *Chapter 1. Economic importance of collateral*—Discuss the principles underlying the economic importance of secured transactions and the gap between the legal framework in the country and best practice. Estimate the potential economic gain to the country from reform. This chapter should motivate nonlegal readers to continue with the chapter on legal problems.

- *Chapter 2. Legal problems*—Identify in precise detail each feature of the law that limits the use or impact of secured transactions at each stage in the process: creation, priority, publicity, and enforcement of a security interest. Trace the microeconomic link between that feature of the law and its economic consequences for collateral and for access to credit. To be convincing to legal readers, this chapter should be fully footnoted with sources in local law.

- *Chapter 3. Economic impact by sector*—Set out the results of the field interviews and additional local data. Many public officials and lawyers will never have discussed the economic impact of legal constraints on secured transactions with business operators in their country. Indeed, for many government officials this chapter will be their first exposure to the pervasive effect of these legal constraints on credit in their own country.

- *Chapter 4. Options for reform*—Discuss the main options for improving the legal system and the filing system.

The field interviews will generate the data on terms for secured and unsecured loans needed for the diagnostic work—data that are difficult to get in any other way (bank websites may provide a backup source, but most banks still do not publish all terms on their website). These data include:

- Spreads over mortgage rates for loans secured by small real estate holdings, movable property, and unsecured loans.
- Customary loan limits on debt service relative to cash flow.
- Terms of car loans compared with those of unsecured loans for similar borrowers.
- Exact terms of mortgage loans, car loans, and personal loans.
- Loan-value ratios for on-road vehicles compared with those for off-road vehicles and other equipment.

Team economists should examine spreads over mortgage rates for loans secured by small real estate holdings, movable property, and unsecured loans. They should check for credit rationing by examining the maturities and customary loan limits on debt service relative to cash flow for unsecured loans, and loans secured by new cars, other movable property, and real estate. They should collect information on the interest rate on each type of loan and whether there are additional limits placed on loans—for example, four years to repay, 12 percent interest rate, debt service never more than 35 percent of income, and total loan never more than $20,000. This information, together with bank lending guidelines on debt service relative to cash flow, makes it possible to determine how loan size changes with collateral.

Data on the use of collateral by banks have some value. In addition to the banks themselves, the superintendent of banks may be able to supply such data. If banks have made loans secured by movable property to individuals who do not own real estate, that shows some confidence in the system. Teasing out this information is difficult, however, because banks often do not record ownership of real estate in their loan statistics unless the real estate is formally mortgaged. The individual loan documents would have to be examined, a task beyond the budget of most projects. Also instructive is a failure to use movable property as collateral. But even when banks do take movable property as collateral, it is often simply to "dress up" unsecured loans.

Macroeconomic data will be important in calculating the potential overall gain from reform. Data on the ratio of private credit to GDP suggest the possible impact of collateral reform. But because these ratios depend on many financial sector and macroeconomic characteristics, they do not by themselves clinch the links between legal problems, limited use of collateral, and limited access to credit. Data on private credit should be confirmed with the central bank. The International Monetary Fund's data on private credit, though widely used, are not collected using uniform definitions. Data on interest rates on the government's hard currency borrowing in foreign markets will be helpful in quantifying country risk. For example, the yield on the government's five-year dollar bonds minus the yield on the U.S. government's five-year dollar bonds will give readers some perspective on the relative payoffs from macroeconomic stabilization and secured transactions reform in terms of interest rate reductions.

The World Bank Group's Doing Business project offers interesting and useful ratings of secured lending systems, and its Enterprise Surveys provide invaluable data on collateral restrictions and demand for collateral by lenders (see the discussion of these data sources in chapter 6). These data sources can help in preparing useful comparisons between the country and comparators. Such comparisons should be presented in the diagnostic study, augmented where possible with findings from the field mission.

PREPARING AND PRESENTING THE DRAFT LAW

In preparing the draft law, the project moves from the diagnostic stage to the actual reform. The drafting of the law will require an expanding circle of local lawyers to check that the proposed reform is consistent with local law and to explain local law. The check for consistency does not mean that the secured transactions reform should be sacrificed to prevailing legal forms. But when derogations of local laws are required for consistency, local lawyers will be best equipped to identify all conflicting laws and warn about public policy issues or special interests that must be handled in the derogation.

The content of the law is fundamental to the reform (for the key elements of a reformed law, including provisions for the filing archive, see chapter 4). To be economically effective, the law must remove the legal restraints on the use of collateral. And to help build consensus in support of the reform, the law must assure stakeholders that it will alleviate their problems. Building consensus also requires attention to several important tactical and presentational issues.

TIMING OF PRESENTATION

The best time to present the draft law is shortly after the government and stakeholders review the diagnostic study. The study typically produces a great deal of agreement, especially flowing from the analysis of legal problems and the field interviews. The law is another matter. The draft forces stakeholders to focus on what must be changed to solve the problems. Sharp questions and opposition should be expected.

DRAFTING COMMITTEE

The project team should prepare a draft of the law before going to the drafting committee. Otherwise, winnowing out issues will be a long and contentious process.

The drafting committee can serve as a forum for the core group of local lawyers to continue working through details of the law. It also provides a place for lawyers representing stakeholders and the government to raise concerns or listen to discussions of issues. And it provides a training ground for the local lawyers whom the project will need in the end to explain issues to their organizations and counterparts. As the team chooses additional local lawyers to participate, it should expect to pay them. The committee's makeup should be ad hoc and flexible, including members sent at the request of the government and private stakeholders as well as those chosen by the original team.

The drafting committee should go over the draft law article by article, suggesting changes and raising questions. Careful minutes should be kept about who attended meetings and how objections were resolved. That will reduce backtracking from agreed positions and permit the drafting committee to move ahead steadily even as membership changes.

Foreign experts in secured transactions law must attend and essentially chair these meetings. That can get expensive. One solution that worked in several projects is to convene drafting committees by conference call, using speakerphones. The draft law can be both transmitted by Internet and projected on the meeting room wall locally. Discussion can proceed paragraph by paragraph, with changes being made as the discussion goes on. In some projects these meetings take place as often as two or three times a week, especially as the time for legislative review approaches. Teleconferencing, if within the team's reach, works even better.

The role of the drafting committee will depend on the project and the position of the donor in the legislative process. Where the World Bank or the International Monetary Fund places the full weight of conditionality on passage of a satisfactory law, the drafting committee may play a secondary role. Where donors must persuade the government to move ahead with reform without the carrot of a large loan or the stick of conditionality, drafting committees can serve as venues for resolving problems in the presence of government officials and key legislators, building confidence in the viability of the proposed reform.

COMMENTARIES

The draft will be a law of great complexity, and it will reverse much of what local lawyers have been taught is correct. Defenders and attackers alike will revisit the same passages many times to understand them and discuss whether other drafting strategies or institutions might better achieve the same results.

The project team and foreign experts will not always be present to answer questions. Detailed commentaries can fill that gap.[1]

The most useful commentaries set out the economic objectives of each important section, comparing, where important, the economic merits of different drafting strategies. If the work of the drafting committee revealed substantial controversy about the draft, the commentaries can also discuss why different drafting options were not taken. The diagnostic study will have set out some of the economic motivation for the details of the draft law, and the commentaries can draw on this material and should otherwise be consistent with it. But the commentaries should be more detailed, to ensure that those examining the law understand the objectives and motivation of the drafting strategy. As the draft law is circulated and discussed, reviewers and discussants will raise more points. Responses to these points should be added to the commentaries.

Commentaries can help preserve vital elements of a draft law. The natural tendency of those reviewing any law is to strike out or simplify language that seems redundant or contrary to good local legal practice. This is a good instinct and should be encouraged. But without good commentaries, reviewers might eliminate legal passages with important economic impact. In Uzbekistan, which received three draft laws in 10 years under different donor-funded projects, Central Bank staff carefully reconstructed each law in a matrix showing parallel clauses. Handwritten comments amounting to "Why?" or "Not consistent with Uzbek law" were sprinkled everywhere. The few remaining points of agreement would have had no economic impact. Good commentaries avoid this reaction by explaining the relevance of each important passage.

The commentaries (and presentations) should pay particular attention to the proposals for enforcement—private enforcement, private sale, and ex parte court orders. Proposals for speeding up enforcement will be the most consistently contentious part of the legal reform. Some opposition can be eliminated by separating the enforcement of consensual security interests from other legal actions that result in the seizure and sale of property. Equally important are the commentaries and repeated proofs of the economic cost of slower systems. But some opposition will remain. Compromises here can be fatal to the economic impact of the law: even a law that clearly directs the judge to order immediate enforcement when the debtor fails to pay can lead to a process long enough to deprive property of much of its value as collateral.

Emphasizing the economic logic of drafting choices can do much to defuse potentially fierce but fruitless doctrinal disputes. Those who object to the draft law can be challenged to come up with drafting solutions that are more compatible with local legal traditions yet still achieve the same economic impact. If they can, those solutions should be adopted. If they can come close, the project economists should weigh the loss in effectiveness against the gain in reduced political opposition.

Suggestions to drop the annotations should be resisted until the government counterpart demands this. If the final law drops these commentaries, as is required in some legislative systems, the now unofficial annotated draft should continue to be circulated so that it can serve as a guide to interpretation of the law for judges and practitioners.

THE FILING ARCHIVE

A well-designed reform will include regulations for the filing archive. That will prevent the archive from becoming a constraint on the reform. The problem of how best to design the filing archive has many reasonable solutions that embody the key principles (see chapter 4). Once the form is decided, the operation of the archive should be clearly set out in the regulations so that the archive does not change into something else. If the proposal calls for an Internet-based filing archive, as is best, directing local stakeholders to other such archives or even setting up a model filing archive for their inspection can be helpful in building support.

The filing archive can be a contentious issue. Unless it is clear that the new archive will be in exactly the same "bureaucratic place" as the old filing system, the officials in charge of the existing registration process may oppose the reform. This opposition should not be taken lightly. In some countries, such as Bolivia and Nicaragua, the registry is a big source of income for the judiciary. In one country a justice minister held up the disbursement of a $100 million tranche of a World Bank loan for a year while negotiating the justice ministry's share in the filing fees. The prospect of major job losses for state employees may also cause officials to oppose the reform. Consider the difference between the more than 1,000 employees of El Salvador's unreformed registry and the 1 supervisory employee of Romania's filing archive. The potential for such big changes in staffing can raise big objections.

Task managers should expect to spend a great deal of time bargaining with their counterpart over the location and fee structure of the registry. Where the registry is in politically powerful hands—such as the supreme court or an independent registry authority—the task manager will have to balance conditionality, disbursement of the loan, and damage to the underlying reform. That will require close coordination with the lawyers and economists on the team. In one project the task manager settled on a high fixed fee to be paid to the ministry of justice in order to permit operation of an efficient, modern system. In another, the task manager permitted the ministry to charge a fixed percentage of the loans secured in the archive, an approach potentially more damaging to the reform.

BUILDING PUBLIC AWARENESS AND MOBILIZING SUPPORT

An economist might imagine that winning broad public acceptance of a new law of secured transactions would be simple. Implementing the reform is fast and cheap. The reform produces a large public gain by reducing the cost of risk management. It leads to broad gains, not gains for some and losses for others. And even where the poor gain, the reform produces large gains for the rich and powerful.

Despite all that, secured transactions reform turns out to be contentious and, judging by the small number of successful reforms, difficult to put into place. How did the successful reform projects win the day? By building on the constituencies that support reform and slowly chipping away at the sources of opposition.

The important interest groups will be quickly identified during the fact-finding and review for the diagnostic study and draft law. All the economic interest groups need to understand how the law will help them. The more specific the analysis, the more useful it will be. Much of this discussion ideally will appear in the diagnostic study. But the dialogue with interest groups should begin when the project team discusses the diagnostic study with those who contributed to it during the first round of interviews. And it should continue when the draft law is presented to these groups for discussion and review.

PRIVATE LENDERS AND SELLERS ON CREDIT

Successful business operators rarely look much beyond their business. So it helps if the diagnostic study has a section on how the law will help them. Including both a section on tractor dealers and a section on car dealers may seem redundant to project staff used to generalization, but it will not seem so to these businesses. Even after the study is circulating, brief notes targeting key groups can be very helpful.

Comparative studies can often be persuasive. A presentation to Ukrainian farmers contrasted the financing of wheat farming in the United States with that in Ukraine. One in Nicaragua compared the use of coffee as collateral in that country with the use of the same coffee as collateral after it was exported to the United States. One donor had another clever idea: sending a Bulgarian television crew to interview U.S. car and equipment dealers on their sale terms. U.S. dealers reacted incredulously to the suggestion that someone wanting to buy a car on credit would have to have title to a condominium. This technique was far more effective than a written analysis in raising questions about prevailing practice in Bulgaria.

DEBTORS AND BORROWERS

Debtors and borrowers usually show strong support for the reform. Lenders normally support it for obvious reasons. Debtors and borrowers do because they have such limited access to credit that the prospect of getting more outweighs the prospect of greater enforcement effort on the debt they already owe.

Sometimes, though, the task manager must deal with important exceptions. In countries where state-operated lenders have been particularly active and politically powerful people have accumulated many bad debts, those debtors may not want to see the debt collection system strengthened. Resigned wisdom teaches that in these circumstances getting a new law will require grandfathering the outstanding debt so that the debt collection system applies only to new debt.

Similarly, in countries undergoing financial crises many borrowers are insolvent and do not want to see stronger debt collection systems. Since only the rich and powerful can get credit, this opposition will be transmitted to the government and the sponsoring donor. Moreover, under the supervisory arrangements typical in such countries, commercial banks will be allowed to "evergreen" their loans to disguise those in default. In these situations even the banks may not strongly support the strengthening of the collection system. Only two paths are politically feasible: grandfathering the outstanding debt or waiting until after the inevitable recapitalization of the banks.

Opposition from private lenders may relate to the prospect of more competition. Sometimes this opposition comes from banks, which are comfortable with high spreads and smaller credit volumes and uninterested in more competition, especially from nonbank lenders. Sometimes the opposition comes from microlenders, which see the ability to securitize unsecured loans not as a benefit that will reduce their costs but as a threat that will increase microlending by other financial institutions.

THE GOVERNMENT

Governments do not always support secured transactions reform. The reason for this varies. Sometimes it is general insensitivity to the needs of the private sector. Sometimes it is a political stake in government-funded lending programs and guarantees, or a desire to protect state-run enterprises or debtors of state lenders from more effective debt collection (box 5.2). But most often lack of government support seems to arise from a failure to understand the logic of the reform or from disbelief that something the government has worried about so much—limits on access to credit—could be explained by legal problems it has not worried about at all.

Special problems sometimes arise with projects run through the ministry of justice. Given enough lead time, working with the ministry of justice as a counterpart appears to have succeeded in some reforms—though lack of evaluations of these reforms makes a final judgment difficult. Justice ministries often do not want to take the lead on what they see as economic reform laws, out of concern that it will open them to attack from the economic ministries on matters of substance and turf. And justice ministries sometimes have vested interests in retaining control over obsolete registration systems that generate fees and, sometimes, rents. Better counterparts tend to be the economic ministries, the superintendent of banks, or the central bank.

But these are generalizations, and there have been exceptions. One is the highly successful reform in Romania, where the Ministry of Justice served as the counterpart. Moreover, this general guidance is no substitute for careful collaboration among the task manager, the foreign experts, and the local team in selecting the counterpart that will champion the reform.

As difficult as the government may be to work with, in the end passing laws is a monopoly of the government. If no one in the government champions the reform, the law will not be presented and the reform will not take place.

LAWYERS AND NOTARIES

Lawyers and notaries sometimes oppose the reform and sometimes support it. Where they oppose it, experience suggests that their opposition is rarely

BOX 5.2

How the political dividends from state-run credit programs can block reform

Where systems for secured transactions are unreformed, state-run and state-guaranteed credit programs can pay huge political dividends. Consider the case of one country with a secured transactions reform on the table: There was broad support among the private groups consulted during the diagnostic study and the drafting of the law. The results of the work were reported in several local law journals, sent by messenger to the ministries of finance and economy, and supported by public resolution of a local bar association. Congressional representatives introduced the draft law in Congress.

Yet despite all this, no government executive agency endorsed the reform project. Nor did any executive agency review the project or raise public policy objections to it. This stance was maintained over the tenures of two different ministers of economy and ministers of finance.

Meanwhile, the same government borrowed $200 million from a multilateral development bank to fund a credit line to be administered by its state-owned bank. The government justified this move on the grounds that private lenders would not make the socially necessary loans to sustain the agricultural sector—loans for livestock, equipment, and fertilizer.

In fact, private lenders would not make those loans because the defective framework for secured transactions made loans secured by such property extremely risky. For that same reason the state-run bank was unable to collect some 30 percent of the loans—representing a $60 million loss.

Why would a government choose a program that led to a loss of $60 million while refusing to act on a project that would have a far greater impact on the economy for a cost of far less than $1 million? Broad domestic support for the credit program cannot explain the choice: the citizens, through their taxes, have to repay the $200 million loan to the multilateral development bank; the $60 million loss is theirs.

The real reason? Observers in the field explained that the executive, by directing the loans from the state-run bank, can achieve important political objectives. After all, even a loan that must be repaid to a state-run bank is a bargain compared with a loan at market rates; for the borrowers who will not repay the $60 million, the gain is even greater. But with reform of the secured transactions law, private citizens would no longer need political favors to get access to credit.

Some politicians will stick to the policies that maximize their incumbency, not the policies that serve the long-term public interest.

based on narrow self-interest, despite the prospect of lower fees. Most professionals see that it does little good to charge a high fee for filing a pledge if no lender will use the instrument.

Most important in winning the support of this group is persuading its members that the proposed legal changes are philosophically consistent with the main body of the country's laws and likely to yield a large economic benefit. A good diagnostic study and clear annotations in the draft law—produced through close collaboration among good local lawyers, foreign legal experts, and economists—are crucial here. The greater the role the local team can play in this work, the easier it becomes to win support among lawyers and notaries.

THE LEGISLATURE

Relations with a country's legislature—its congress or parliament—present both opportunities and challenges. Committees dealing with relevant issues are usually quick to see the need for the reform and can become valuable allies. But multilateral institutions face constraints in their direct dealings with a legislature because of their understandings with the administrative branch, which often does not like these institutions to "go behind its back." Creative collaboration with European and North American donors that are less constrained can be one way to get around this. Sometimes these donors have consultative arrangements in place that include the legislature, and these can serve as neutral territory for explaining proposals.

Even when the administration supports the law, however, it often cannot defend it before the legislature because it lacks staff with the necessary skills or understanding. The project therefore needs resources for presenting and responding to this body. This is a step often neglected by multilateral institutions, used to dealing only with the administrative branch. Such support can keep otherwise well-meaning legislators from simply chopping off parts of a reform law because of a failure to understand their relationship with the overall reform.

Individual legislators typically understand and support the reform. They are often much closer to the private sector than the administration is, and they have an interest in being responsive to their constituencies. But sustaining their support in the face of larger political issues is a common problem.

THE CENTRAL BANK OR SUPERINTENDENT OF BANKS

Improving the legal framework for debt collection might be expected to bear closely on the main concerns of a central bank or superintendent of banks. Yet in the countries that have undertaken secured transactions reform, these entities have never initiated the reform program, though they have sometimes strongly supported it.[2] This lack of a clear pattern of support stems in part from the same factors that lead administration attitudes.

So task managers should not take the support of the central bank or superintendent of banks for granted, should lobby to get it, and should have a plan for working around opposition if it should develop.

WEIGHING WHEN TO COMPROMISE

When to compromise? A key principle to keep in mind: The less compromise, the greater the economic impact of the reform. Still, different compromises produce different amounts of harm. The economist and the foreign legal expert should advise on how much harm would come from a compromise. The task manager can then weigh the change in economic impact against the change in political opposition and decide whether the compromise is worth it.

Some compromises produce continuous harm. For example, each increase in the filing fee acts as a tax on the system and reduces secured lending. The higher the fee, the less effective the reform. Moreover, an escalation in fees hurts the borrowers with the lowest-value collateral, precisely those most likely to be members of groups often targeted by donors. Nonetheless, a higher fee need not destroy the reform. In at least one case a higher fee "bought off" a key government agency that had opposed the reform, paving the way forward.

Some compromises leave part of the reform in place, reducing effectiveness by discrete amounts. For example, reforming the company act in a common law country and confining the reform to loans made by corporations could produce a workable subsystem. Of course, that subsystem would exclude perhaps 90 percent of the economic units operating in the country, including farmers, micro and small enterprises, and most businesses operated by the poor—all groups targeted by multilateral development bank activity. These exclusions would substantially reduce the economic effectiveness of the reform. But the subsystem is one that could operate independently. Another subsystem that could be workable is one confined to a certain type of collateral. Ukraine had a system that permitted secured lending only for new cars, and Nepal a system that permitted secured lending only against jewelry brought to the Central Bank. Since cars and gold represent only a small share of capital, such a system would have limited economic impact. But within its narrow scope it could work.

Other compromises are more lethal. No first-to-file priority rule? Super-priority for government tax liens? Three-year court enforcement periods? Court-administered sale procedures that absorb all the value of the collateral? A forest of potentially inconsistent laws to establish priority? No public access to the filing archive? These compromises will destroy the reform and, since the resources invested in the reform are not costless, result in a net loss. To inform decisions on these issues, the project economists should supply ongoing estimates of the cost of departures from the ideal reform.

NOTES

1. One example of a draft law with commentaries is Romania's. See Nuria de la Peña and Heywood Fleisig, "Romania: Law on Security Interests in Personal Property and Commentaries," *Review of Central and East European Law* 29, no. 2 (2004): 133–217.

2. At a 1997 International Monetary Fund seminar that brought together central bank counsels, no counsel or IMF staff member in attendance was able to identify any steps that the counsel or the government had taken to improve the framework for secured lending.

CHAPTER 6

MONITORING AND EVALUATING THE REFORM

Measuring results is a key part of secured transactions reform, for several reasons. First, all the important effects of the reform on lending terms and volumes should be readily measurable. Second, allocating donor resources effectively requires knowing what works. And third, measurement supports and focuses the dialogue with stakeholders. When everyone knows that results, not doctrinal purity, will be the measure of success, it becomes easier to tally the cost of compromise and to manage that cost.

MEASURING ECONOMIC GAIN USING MODEL-BASED INDICATORS

In principle, determining the success of a secured transactions reform is straightforward: Can property be used as collateral, and does that use lead to better loan terms for borrowers? The success of a reform can also be measured in the economic gain it produces.

The economic gain from the new system comes from larger volumes of credit and lower interest rates. Figure 6.1 shows a stylized version of this gain. Before the reform, lenders offer different amounts of credit at different interest rates. They offer mortgages at rate r-1 up to an amount that can be no greater than 80 percent of the value of land and buildings. They offer loans secured by automobiles at rate r-2 up to an amount that cannot exceed about 90 percent of the value of the stock of automobiles. Finally, they offer unsecured loans at rate r-3, with the total amount of credit constrained by the features of the loan market discussed in previous chapters. Borrowers can invest these funds at the rates of return shown by the curve for the marginal product of capital (MPK); derived from the country's production function, this curve shows the return to investors from additional units of capital. Thus the vertical distance between the borrowing rate and the MPK is the net profit of borrowers, the economic gain from the (unreformed) system.

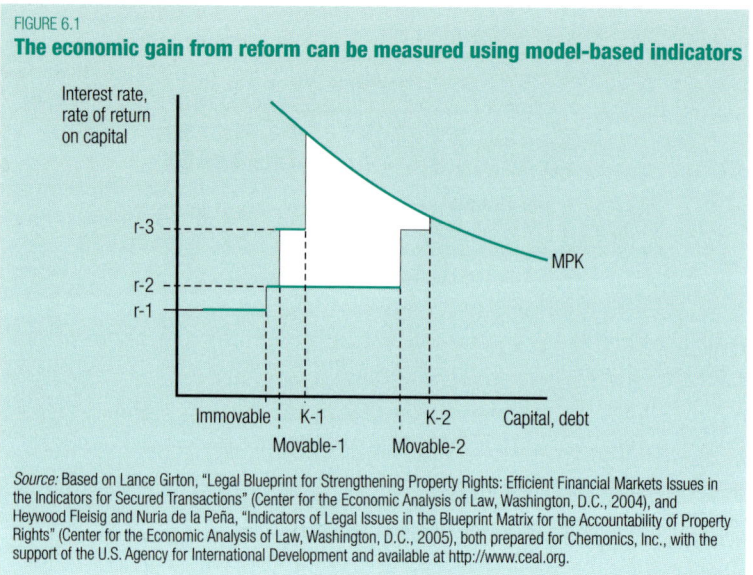

FIGURE 6.1

The economic gain from reform can be measured using model-based indicators

Source: Based on Lance Girton, "Legal Blueprint for Strengthening Property Rights: Efficient Financial Markets Issues in the Indicators for Secured Transactions" (Center for the Economic Analysis of Law, Washington, D.C., 2004), and Heywood Fleisig and Nuria de la Peña, "Indicators of Legal Issues in the Blueprint Matrix for the Accountability of Property Rights" (Center for the Economic Analysis of Law, Washington, D.C., 2005), both prepared for Chemonics, Inc., with the support of the U.S. Agency for International Development and available at http://www.ceal.org.

After the reform, both the amount of credit secured by movable property and the total amount of credit rise. Lending secured by movable property rises from "movable-1" to "movable-2" at interest rate r-2. Total credit rises from K-1 to K-2.

Borrowers now get the difference between the return on capital (MPK) and the interest rate r-2 on a larger amount of credit, increasing their total gain from the (now reformed) system. The analysis assumes, for the sake of simplicity, that neither the mortgage nor the unsecured lending regime changes. The gain from the reform is the difference between the total gain from the system less the gain from the unreformed system (shown in white). That equals the shaded area. As a rough approximation, the gain equals the increase in the volume of secured credit times the difference in interest rates between unsecured loans and loans secured by movable property. A closer approximation is the difference between the MPK and the lending rate secured by movable property times the increase in lending secured by movable property. That measure would require some information about the production function.[1]

For some purposes (such as project evaluation) the absolute gain will be the relevant measure; for others (such as cross-country comparisons) the gain should be standardized by GDP or total credit outstanding. The measure of gain can also serve as an indicator of the efficiency of the system, allowing

Table 6.1
DATA REQUIREMENTS FOR MEASURING IMPACT OF REFORM

Indicator	Loans secured by real estate		Loans secured by new vehicles		Loans secured by used vehicles		Unsecured loans	
	Before reform	**After reform**	**Before reform**	**After reform**	**Before reform**	**After reform**	**Before reform**	**After reform**
Volume of credit								
Ratio of loan to property value								
Interest rate								
Limit on loan size								

comparison of the actual situation with postreform potential. The worst system would have the largest cost, relative to GDP.

Despite the potential simplicity of this approach to measuring the gain from reform, no donor has undertaken such an evaluation of past projects. Consequently, no accurate comparison exists of the effectiveness of different approaches to reform. This shortcoming, regrettably, also applies to the advice in this book.

Best practice in reform projects calls for gathering the full range of data needed to measure impact. For a relatively complete evaluation the data required include the volume of loans and the interest rate by type of collateral both before and after reform (table 6.1). Data should be gathered for the four main types of loans: loans secured by immovable property, by new motor vehicles, and by used motor vehicles and unsecured loans. For unsecured loans careful attention should be paid to requirements that the borrower own real estate or have the cosignature of an owner of real estate or a supervisor in a government job.

What would indicate a successful reform? The interest rate spreads between loans secured by real estate and both loans secured by movable property and unsecured loans should fall. The rates on loans secured by movable property should improve relative to mortgage rates because the value of movable property as collateral should improve relative to the value of fixed property as collateral. And the rates on unsecured loans should fall relative to mortgage rates because the new framework should enable unsecured lenders to use portfolios of unsecured loans as collateral for refinancing loans.

The most difficult task lies in determining how much lending terms for loans secured by other movable property have improved relative to the terms for motor vehicles. Such terms are not readily available to the public (though terms for car loans are often posted on the Internet). One option is to reinterview lenders and sellers on credit. But projects typically do not support such ex post investigations. Natural sources for these data are the World Bank Group's Enterprise Surveys or other rigorously implemented firm-level surveys. Otherwise, some inferences can be made from data collected from the filing archive and by the central bank.

MEASURING GAINS USING DATA FROM FILING ARCHIVES

One measure of results that approaches the ideal was produced by the European Bank for Reconstruction and Development, which computed filings per capita for several filing archives in Central and Eastern Europe. The results give an immediate measure of the increase in the number of secured loans after reform (figure 6.2).

The EBRD results are the most powerful evidence available of the importance of secured transactions reform in expanding loan volumes. Still, a change in the number of secured loans does not necessarily show that the value of secured loans has increased—nor does it show the base from which they started or how much the interest rate declined. Moreover, even if a reform does not increase the number of filings, that does not mean that it failed: if the existing number of filings is large, the decline in the interest rate on the existing stock of loans will produce a gain proportionate to the size of that decline.

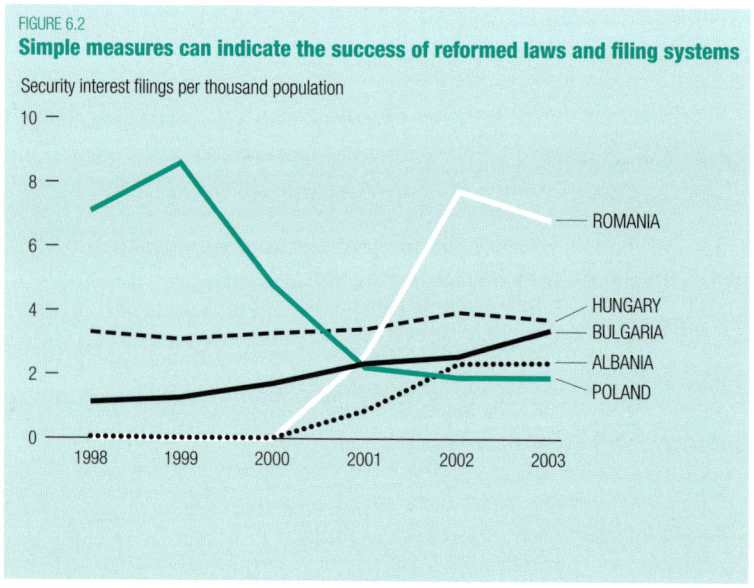

FIGURE 6.2
Simple measures can indicate the success of reformed laws and filing systems

Security interest filings per thousand population

An EBRD presentation of the findings conservatively describes them as indicating only the efficiency of the filing systems.[2] That characterization understates the importance of the EBRD data: they go some way toward evaluating the impact of the overall reform. The EBRD's work is an imaginative effort that advances the debate on secured transactions reform. A simple study of the impact of the Romanian reform shows how effectiveness can be measured using statistics from filing archives combined with loan data from the Central Bank.[3] The evaluation shows that in the first four years of operation the reform led to 600,000 filings and generated sustainable credit of at least $60 million, at a project cost of less than $1 million. (The study lacked funding to collect interest rates.) The economic impact was broad: filings occurred for the first time or rose in every county in Romania—and they rose in both rural and urban areas and for smaller loan sizes (presumably indicating greater access to credit among lower-income borrowers). Consistent with this, private credit rose from 10 percent of GDP to 15 percent over the four-year period.

ASSESSING ACCESS TO CREDIT USING ENTERPRISE SURVEY DATA

An excellent source of information on a variety of topics related to secured transactions reform is the firms themselves. The World Bank Group's Enterprise Surveys (and other firm-level surveys implemented with rigor) provide a range of useful firm-level information: how firms finance working capital and fixed investment, what property is acceptable to lenders as collateral for their loans, to what extent firms are rationed out of the market because collateral requirements are too stringent.[4] Where surveys take place both before and after reform, they can provide important information about changes in access to credit.

Data based on firms' responses to several sets of questions, available for almost all Enterprise Surveys, can highlight challenges to and opportunities from strengthening the legal framework for secured transactions:

- *Sources of financing.* Where do firms obtain financing for their working capital needs (inventories, accounts receivable) and new investments (purchases of land, buildings, machinery, or equipment)? The possible sources listed in the survey include retained earnings, commercial banks, leasing companies, development finance, trade credit, and credit cards. A secured transactions reform would be expected to increase trade credit and leasing credit, since it would make both types of contracts more attractive.
- *Characteristics of loans.* For firms with loans from financial institutions, the surveys ask a range of questions: Did the loan require collateral? What type of collateral was required (land or buildings, immovable plant,

machinery, movable machinery, household property, other intangible assets)? What was the value of the collateral as a percentage of the loan value? How was the loan used (to buy machinery, fixed assets, inputs)?

■ *Credit rationing.* For firms without loans from financial institutions, the surveys ask whether they applied for a loan but were denied, or whether they simply did not apply. If they were turned down, what was the main reason given (lack of acceptable collateral, bad credit history)? If they chose not to apply, what was the reason? These data can be used to measure the degree to which firms are rationed out of the credit market because their assets do not match the collateral requirements.

■ *Firms' asset portfolios.* One indicator in particular, movable assets as a percentage of the book value of a firm, can demonstrate the extent of the mismatch between the assets that most small firms have and the property that formal sector lenders will accept as collateral.

Data from the Enterprise Surveys provide several possible indicators of success. One is an increase in loans secured by movable property relative to loans secured by real estate. Another is an increase in access to credit by firms without large amounts of fixed assets.

Not all countries have had Enterprise Surveys. For these, other firm-level surveys may be worth consulting. It may even be worthwhile to implement a short firm-level survey to get benchmark figures on collateral and movable assets. These data could allow comparisons with "good practice" countries and help show the opportunity costs to the private sector of failing to undertake the reform.

ASSESSING LENDERS' TRANSACTION COSTS USING DOING BUSINESS INDICATORS

A good source of information on the lenders' side is the World Bank Group's Doing Business project, which relies on surveys of experts.[5] For lenders the project measures the transaction costs of lending: the time and cost incurred by banks and nonbank financial institutions in extending secured credit. The Doing Business indicators include information on:

■ Cost to create collateral.
■ Legal rights index (reflects the legal rights of borrowers and lenders, measuring the degree to which collateral and bankruptcy laws facilitate lending).[6]
■ Number of procedures to enforce collateral.
■ Time (in days) to enforce contracts.
■ Cost (as a percentage of debt) to enforce collateral.

These indicators are particularly valuable in the diagnostic phase. In some cases it will be easy to see why lenders typically do not take security interests in movable property, as in Argentina, where the Doing Business indicators illustrate the enormous cost and time associated with enforcing collateral (figure 6.3). This type of analysis is useful both to benchmark changes in the legal framework over time and to catalyze a discussion on the need for change in

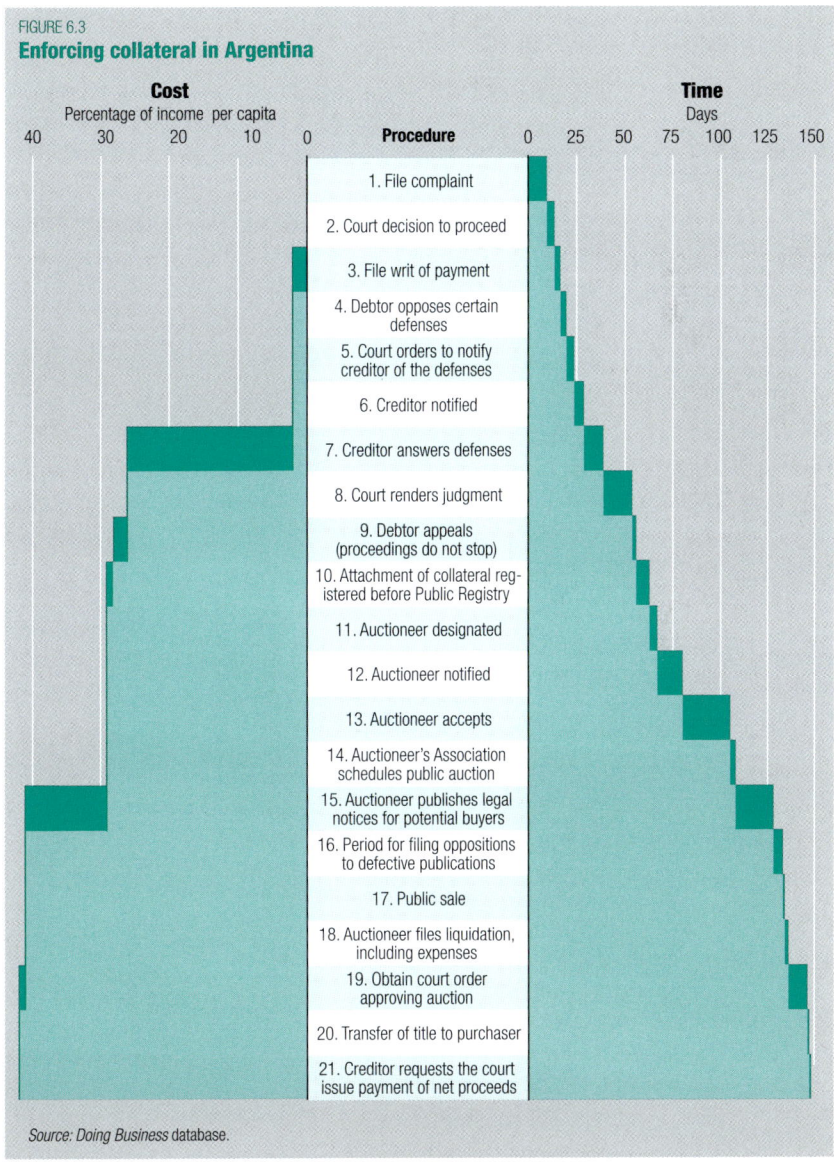

FIGURE 6.3
Enforcing collateral in Argentina

Source: Doing Business database.

the first place. The indicators are also excellent benchmarking tools: the Doing Business project provides such wide coverage of countries that cross-country comparisons are fairly straightforward, making it easy for a project team to show a country how it compares with its neighbors, key global competitors, or good practice countries.

Where pre- and postreform data are available, they can give some measure of the qualitative success of reform. But to judge the impact, the team must rely on the model-based indicators that measure the economic gain from the increased credit.

NOTES

1. For a discussion of the derivation of this model, an alternative treatment based on transaction costs, and references to applications, see the sources cited for figure 6.1. For a discussion of the need for model-based indicators, see Heywood Fleisig, Neil Roger, and Syed Mahmood, "Project Performance and Development Impact Indicators for Projects in Private Sector Development: A First Edition Note" (World Bank, Private Sector Development Department, Washington, D.C., 1995; available at http://www.ceal.org).

2. Frédérique Dahan, "EBRD Guiding Principles for the Development of Charges (Collateral) Registry," paper presented at World Bank Brown Bag Lunch (Washington, D.C., May 17, 2005; European Bank for Reconstruction and Development, London).

3. Rodrigo Chaves, Heywood Fleisig, and Nuria de la Peña, "Secured Transactions Reform: Early Results from Romania," CEAL Issues Brief (Center for the Economic Analysis of Law, Washington, D.C., 2004).

4. Data from Enterprise Surveys are available at http://rru.worldbank.org/ EnterpriseSurveys/. Not all relevant data are available online. Gaining access to all the data collected by a survey may require consulting with the World Bank Group's Investment Climate Department.

5. Data from the Doing Business project are available at http://rru.worldbank. org/DoingBusiness/.

6. The legal rights index is based on data collected through a study of collateral and insolvency laws, supported by responses to a survey on secured transactions laws. The index includes three aspects relating to legal rights in bankruptcy and seven found in collateral law. It ranges from 0 to 10, with higher scores indicating that collateral and bankruptcy laws are better designed to expand access to credit.

RESOURCES

Several different types of resources are available to task managers to aid in planning and implementing a secured transactions reform project.

BRIEF INTRODUCTIONS TO SECURED TRANSACTIONS AND DEVELOPMENT

These short notes and articles discuss the source of legal barriers to access to credit and the economic impact of these barriers. These summary resources may be particularly useful where brief introductions to the legal and economic issues are needed for discussions with policymakers.

de la Peña, Nuria, and Heywood Fleisig. "SMEs and Collateral." CEAL Issues Brief. Center for the Economic Analysis of Law, Washington, D.C., 2002.

Fleisig, Heywood. "The Power of Collateral: How Problems in Secured Transactions Limit Private Credit for Movable Property." Viewpoint series, Note 43. World Bank Group, Private Sector Development Vice Presidency, Washington, D.C., 1995.

———. "The Right to Borrow: Legal and Regulatory Barriers That Limit Access to Credit by Small Farmers and Businesses." Viewpoint series, Note 44. World Bank Group, Private Sector Development Vice Presidency, Washington, D.C., 1995.

———. "Secured Transactions: The Power of Collateral." *Finance and Development* 33, no. 2 (1996): 44–46. (Available in Arabic, Chinese, French, German, and Spanish.)

Fleisig, Heywood, and Nuria de la Peña. "Microenterprise and Collateral." CEAL Issues Brief. Center for the Economic Analysis of Law, Washington, D.C., 2002.

———. "Why the Microcredit Crunch?" *Microenterprise Development Review* (Inter-American Development Bank) 5, no. 2 (2002). http://www.iadb.org/sds/doc/vol5n2eng.pdf. (Available in Spanish.)

Safavian, Mehnaz, Heywood Fleisig, and Jevgenijs Steinbuks. "Unlocking Dead Capital: How Reforming Collateral Laws Improves Access to Finance." Viewpoint series. World Bank Group, Private Sector Development Vice Presidency, Washington, D.C., forthcoming.

GENERAL REVIEWS OF REFORM IN DEVELOPING AND TRANSITION ECONOMIES

These articles reviewing general issues of reform in developing and transition economies give an additional flavor of how problems can vary among countries with similar legal systems and among different legal systems. Several of the authors have experience in reform efforts.

Dahan, Frédérique, and John Simpson. "The European Bank for Reconstruction and Development's Secured Transactions Project: A Model Law and Ten Core Principles for a Modern Secured Transactions Law in Countries of Central and Eastern Europe (and Elsewhere!)." In Eva-Maria Kieninger, ed., *Security Rights in Movable Property in European Private Law.* Cambridge: Cambridge University Press, 2004.

de la Peña, Nuria, Heywood Fleisig, and Philip Wellons. "Secured Transactions." In *Law and Policy Reform at the Asian Development Bank 2000.* Vol. 2. Manila: Asian Development Bank, 2000. http://www.adb.org/Documents/others/Law_ADB/lpr_2000_2.asp?p=lawdevt.

Garro, Alejando M. "Harmonization of Personal Property Security Law: National, Regional and Global Initiatives." *Uniform Law Review/Revue de droit uniforme* 8 (2003): 357–68.

Norton, Joseph J., and Mads Andenas, eds. *Emerging Financial Markets and Secured Transactions.* The Hague: Kluwer Law International, 1998.

Welsh, Allen. "Secured Transactions Law: Best Practices & Policy Options." Working Paper 03/06. IRIS Center at the University of Maryland, College Park, 2003. http://www.iris.umd.edu/Reader.aspx?TYPE=FORMAL_PUBLICATION&ID=b0ad1ce9-1d11-4a41-a5fb-5740dfbf6600.

LEGAL LITERATURE

Summarizing the vast legal literature on secured lending is beyond the scope of this book. With apologies to those excluded, following is a brief list of useful material. For detailed judgments about the legal aspects of reform, however, task managers should generally depend on specialist lawyers. It is unrealistic to hope to become expert in this area in the normal time frame for executing development projects or in typical tours of duty in staff positions at multilateral institutions.

BRIEF GENERAL GUIDES

Bailey, Henry J., III, and Richard B. Hagedorn. *Secured Transactions in a Nutshell.* 4th ed. St. Paul, Minn.: West Publishing Company, 2000.

Hakes, Russell A. *The ABCs of the UCC, Article 9: Secured Transactions.* Chicago: Section of Business Law, American Bar Association, 1996.

EARLY STUDIES OF AND PROPOSALS FOR REFORM

These comprehensive early studies laid the foundation for the study of the severe defects in the laws on secured transactions in both industrial and developing countries. Aimed at a general legal audience, they often set out a comparative exposition of defects and many fundamental points more clearly than typical law review articles. They also include discussions on the function of the judicial system (such as on contract enforcement and the timeliness of courts).

Garro, Alejandro M. "Recordation in Argentine Law." *Revista Jurídica de la Universidad Interamericana de Puerto Rico* 15 (January–April 1981): 175–221.

————. "Security Interests in Personal Property in Latin America: A Comparison with Article 9 and a Model for Reform." *Houston Journal of International Law* 9 (1987): 157–242.

————. "Unification and Harmonization of Private Law in Latin America." *American Journal of Comparative Law* 40, no. 3 (1992): 587–616.

Kozolchyk, Boris. "Law and the Credit Structure in Latin America." *Virginia Journal of International Law* 7, no. 1 (1967).

————. "Toward a Theory on Law in Economic Development: The Costa Rican USAID-ROCAP Law Reform Project." *Law & Social Order Journal* (Arizona State University) 4 (1971): 681–.

United Nations Commission on International Trade Law (UNCITRAL). "Report of the Secretary-General: Study on Security Interests." In *United Nations Commission on International Trade Law Yearbook Volume VIII: 1977.* New York: United Nations, 1978. A/CN.9/131.

SCHOLARLY REVIEWS

These two articles ponder some of the legal subtleties of the secured transactions framework, offering lawyers' perspectives on the economic issues in secured lending. The issues they explore apply to reform in both industrial and developing countries. Though less accessible than the studies cited in the previous section, the articles contain extensive bibliographies listing similar articles as well as articles discussing individual topics in greater detail.

Scott, Robert E. "A Relational Theory of Secured Financing." *Columbia Law Review* 86 (June 1986): 901–77.

Triantis, George G. "On the Efficiency of Secured Lending." *Virginia Law Review* 80 (1994): 2155–68.

INTERNATIONAL CONVENTIONS AND MODEL LAWS

International organizations, alert to the growing attention being paid to the legal framework for secured lending, have responded with two broad initiatives: international conventions and model laws. Properly used, these can help task managers design a reform project and get support for it.

International conventions are agreements to enforce laws across borders. Model laws are more loosely defined. They may range in generality from instructive principles to guiding frameworks to detailed templates. Instructive principles appear in the World Bank's legal framework for creditor rights and in the United Nations Commission on International Trade Law's (UNCITRAL) forthcoming legislative guide to secured transactions.[1] Guiding frameworks appear in the model laws developed by the European Bank for Reconstruction and Development and by the Organization of American States (OAS).[2] The most detailed template is the U.S. Uniform Commercial Code, Article 9 (UCC9), intended to be adopted nearly verbatim by participating states.[3]

Whatever their applicability in detail to the task facing a task manager, all these efforts can be useful in convincing stakeholders of the importance of reforming secured transactions laws. Even skeptics resistant to reasoned explanation of the effects of such reform might be persuaded by the reform elements set out in these sources and by the attention given to the reform by important institutions.

INTERNATIONAL CONVENTIONS

International conventions bind the signatories. Compromise is therefore integral to the drafting process, making it difficult for conventions to represent best practice. The need to bind different signatories—with varied philosophies and varied constraints—means that those drafting a convention must constantly balance modern drafting principles against the need to achieve broad acceptability.

Still, when a good balance is struck, international conventions can form an important strategic resource for a task manager. One example is the Convention on International Interests in Mobile Equipment, developed under the auspices of the International Institute for the Unification of Private Law (UNIDROIT), which will become the standard for financing aircraft equipment.[4] Many countries that are unaware of the underlying legal reform will nonetheless have a keen interest in gaining access to aircraft finance by acceding to the convention. That interest can become an important point of entry in convincing governments of the importance of reforming the broader laws applying to movable property as collateral. Adding approval of the UNIDROIT convention to the package of laws a task manager submits to a government is a relatively low-cost step that would broaden the appeal of the package beyond the agencies directly supervising the reform.

Another recent international convention relevant to secured finance is the United Nations Convention on the Assignment of Receivables in International Trade, drafted under the auspices of UNCITRAL.[5] Because the drafters were unable to agree on the need to register security interests in accounts receivable or to register transfers of accounts receivable, the convention makes registration optional, undermining the ability to establish priority and make it known to third parties. Therefore, this convention does not so much provide for a new security device as advance important aspects of the commercial law governing accounts receivable. Even so, the convention's focus on accounts receivable can help underscore for skeptical policymakers the concern about these commercially valuable items of movable property among important segments of the world community.[6]

MODEL LAWS

While drafting international conventions requires compromise to resolve international differences in approach, drafting a domestic law of secured transactions usually involves little pressure for international political compromise (except, of course, from donors). That freedom can permit new laws to better reflect best practice. Indeed, the lack of established tradition can enable some developing and transition economies to leapfrog past industrial economies. Romania's law of secured transactions includes all the features of the latest version of Article 9 of the U.S. Uniform Commercial Code plus some other economically desirable features that were politically controversial in the United States but not in Romania.

The EBRD, the first international financial institution to formally endorse the reform of secured transactions law, has led the efforts among such institutions to produce a model law and apply it in the field.[7] Supported by a strong staff over the past decade, its work on a model law has been complemented by many interesting and useful studies and reform projects, some of which are cited in this book.[8] The OAS produced its model law more recently.[9]

These laws are clearly intended to serve only as models, and neither the EBRD nor the OAS law has been enacted anywhere as such. Indeed, both institutions explicitly state that they intend their model law to illustrate principles, not to be enacted.[10] Each designed its model law to be flexible, allowing it to be readily adapted to local political, economic, and legal circumstances.

Article 9 of the U.S. Uniform Commercial Code, the first of the comprehensive functional laws of secured transactions, is also a model law. In the federal structure of the United States, laws governing security interests are the responsibility of each state. So UCC9 serves as a model for the secured transactions laws voluntarily adopted by each of the 50 states. The drafting of UCC9 is organized by nongovernmental organizations (the American Law Institute and the American Bar Association), working with the National Conference of Commissioners on Uniform State Laws.

Of course, any successful law of secured transactions can serve as a model. Such laws would include any of the versions of UCC9, the Canadian Personal Property Security Acts (passed at the provincial level), and the New Zealand Personal Property Securities Act 1999.[11] They would also include any of the recent reform laws in developing countries, of which Romania's seems to be the most successful.[12] Indeed, the very abundance of these laws can help persuade conservative stakeholders that secured transactions reform has been successfully enacted elsewhere.

Model laws cannot be mechanically applied, however. They do not always reflect ideal practice—by which is meant, broadly, a legal framework that will maximize the economic value of property as collateral (see chapter 3). There are no good surveys that analyze the relevance of different model laws in reform efforts, and task managers must depend on the team lawyers and economists to decide which practices would be appropriate for the country undertaking reform.

ECONOMICS LITERATURE

These articles from the economics literature set out most of the main issues relating to the importance of collateral for private financial markets. While the articles raise many important points for consideration, some assume a legal structure for the secured transactions system that does not reflect best practice, limiting the generality of several conclusions.

Allen, Franklin, and Douglas Gale. "Optimal Security Design." *Review of Financial Studies* 1 (1988): 229–63.

Barro, Robert J. "The Loan Market, Collateral, and Rates of Interest." *Journal of Money, Credit, and Banking* 8 (November 1976): 439–56.

Benjamin, Daniel. "The Use of Collateral to Enforce Debt Contracts." *Economic Inquiry* 16 (July 1978): 333–59.

Berger, Allen N., and Gregory F. Udell. "Collateral, Loan Quality and Bank Risk." *Journal of Monetary Economics* 25 (1990): 21–42.

Besanko, David, and Anjan V. Thakor. "Collateral and Rationing: Sorting Equilibria in Monopolistic and Competitive Credit Markets." *International Economic Review* 28 (October 1987): 671–89.

Bester, Helmut. "The Role of Collateral in a Model of Debt Renegotiation." *Journal of Money, Credit, and Banking* 26 (February 1994): 72–85.

———. "The Role of Collateral in Credit Markets with Imperfect Information." *European Economic Review* 31 (1987): 887–99.

———. "Screening versus Rationing in Credit Markets with Imperfect Information." *American Economic Review* 75 (1985): 850–55.

Boot, Arnoud W. A., Anjan V. Thakor, and Gregory F. Udell. "Secured Lending and Default Risk: Equilibrium Analysis, Policy Implications, and Empirical Results." *Economic Journal* 101 (May 1991): 458–72.

Carter, David J., Katherine G. Carman, and Eric D. Pinsky. "Collateral Limitations and Borrower Utility: An Explanation of Welfare Losses under a Dual Punishment System." Center for the Economic Analysis of Law, Washington, D.C., 1995.

Eaton, Jonathan, Mark Gersovitz, and Joseph E. Stiglitz. "The Pure Theory of Country Risk." *European Economic Review* 30 (1986): 481–513.

Gale, Douglas, and Martin Hellwig. "Incentive-Compatible Debt Contracts: The One-Period Problem." *Review of Economic Studies* 52 (1985): 647–63.

Hellwig, Martin. "Bankruptcy, Limited Liability, and the Modigliani-Miller Theorem." *American Economic Review* 71 (1981): 155–70.

———. "Comment on 'The Pure Theory of Country Risk' by Jonathan Eaton, Mark Gersovitz, and Joseph E. Stiglitz." *European Economic Review* 30 (1986): 521–27.

Hellwig, Martin, and Helmut Bester. "Moral Hazard and Equilibrium Credit Rationing: An Overview of the Issues." In Günter Bamberg and Klaus Spremann, eds., *Agency Theory, Information and Incentives.* Heidelberg: Springer-Verlag, 1987.

Leeth, John D., and Jonathan A. Scott. "The Incidence of Secured Debt: Evidence from the Small Business Community." *Journal of Financial and Quantitative Analysis* 24 (1989): 379–93.

Smith, Clifford W., Jr. "Bankruptcy, Secured Debt, and Optimal Capital Structure: Comment." *Journal of Finance* 34 (March 1979): 247–51.

Wette, Hildegard C. "Collateral in Credit Rationing in Markets with Imperfect Information: Note." *American Economic Review* 73 (June 1983): 442–45.

STUDIES INTEGRATING THE LAW AND ECONOMICS OF SECURED TRANSACTIONS IN DEVELOPING AND TRANSITION ECONOMIES

These studies examine the problems in laws of secured transactions and link these legal problems to observed restrictions on access to credit. They also discuss how a limited framework for transactions secured by movable property affects growth and the distribution of wealth and income. Some studies include appendixes measuring the economic costs and benefits of reform of the legal framework for secured transactions.

Bogetic, Zeljko, and Heywood W. Fleisig. "Collateral, Access to Credit, and Investment in Bulgaria." In Derek C. Jones and Jeffrey Miller, eds., *The Bulgarian Economy: Lessons from Reform during Early Transition.* Aldershot, England: Ashgate, 1997.

Corrigan, E. Gerald. "Building Effective Banking Systems in Latin America and the Caribbean: Tactics and Strategy." IFM-107. Inter-American Development Bank, Washington, D.C., 1997.

de la Peña, Nuria. "Mexico: Identificación de los Problemas de Garantías para Financiar Bienes Muebles en El Sector Agropecuario." *El Foro* (Barra de Abogados de Mexico, Mexico City) 9, no. 2 (1996). http://www.bma.org. mx/publicaciones/elforo/1996/2sem/mexico.html.

de la Peña, Nuria, and Heywood W. Fleisig. "Romania: Draft Law on Security Interests in Movable Property with Commentaries" (România: Lege privind Garantiile Reale Mobiliare si Comentarii). Center for the Economic Analysis of Law, Washington, D.C., 1999. (As Law 99 of May 26, 1999, also published in *Monitorul Oficial* 236 [Parlamentul României, Bucharest, May 27, 1999; http://www.monitoruloficial.ro].)

de la Peña, Nuria, and Roberto Muguillo. "Case Disposition Time for Seizing and Selling Movable Property in Capital Federal Commercial Courts." *Estudios de Derecho Comercial: Revista del Instituto de Derecho Comercial, Económico y Empresarial* (Colegio de Abogados de San Isidro, San Isidro, Argentina) 1 (1997).

de la Peña, Nuria, Heywood Fleisig, and Fernando Cantuarias. *Trabas Legales al Acceso a Credito en Perú.* Lima: Universidad Peruana de Ciencias Aplicadas, 2000.

de la Peña, Nuria, Heywood W. Fleisig, and Roberto Muguillo. "Argentina: Anteproyecto de Ley de Garantías Reales Muebles." *Estudios de Derecho Comercial: Revista del Instituto de Derecho Comercial, Económico y Empresarial* (Colegio de Abogados de San Isidro, San Isidro, Argentina) (April 1998).

de la Peña, Nuria, Heywood W. Fleisig, Alejandro M. Garro, and Roberto Muguillo. *Costo Económico de los Defectos en el Marco Legal Argentino para los Créditos con Garantía de Bienes Muebles.* Vol. 2 of *Poder Judicial, Desarrollo Económico y Competitividad en la Argentina.* Buenos Aires: Editorial Depalma for FORES and CONICET, 2001.

Fleisig, Heywood W., and Nuria de la Peña. "Argentina: Cómo las Leyes para Garantizar Prestamos Limitan el Acceso a Crédito." *La Ley* (Buenos Aires) 61, no. 47 (March 7, 1997): 1–2.

———. "Peru: How Problems in the Framework for Secured Transactions Limit Access to Credit." *NAFTA: Law and Business Review of the Americas* (Southern Methodist University, Dallas) 3 (1997): 33–72.

Fleisig, Heywood, Juan Carlos Aguilar, and Nuria de la Peña. "Economic Cost of Deficiencies in Bolivia's Collateral Law." In World Bank, "How Legal Restrictions on Collateral Limit Access to Credit in Bolivia." Report 13873-BO. Latin America and the Caribbean Region, Office of the Chief Economist, Washington, D.C., 1994.

———. "Results of an Analysis of Bolivian Debt Collection Cases." In World Bank, "How Legal Restrictions on Collateral Limit Access to Credit in Bolivia." Report 13873-BO. Latin America and the Caribbean Region, Office of the Chief Economist, Washington, D.C., 1994.

Fleisig, Heywood W., John Simpson, and Jan-Hendrik Rover. "No Loans for Movable Property?" In World Bank, *World Development Report 1996: From Plan to Market.* New York: Oxford University Press, 1996.

Galindo, Arturo. "Creditor Rights and the Credit Market: Where Do We Stand?" Research Department Working Paper 448. Inter-American Development Bank, Washington, D.C., 2001.

Kozolchyk, Boris. "What to Do about Mexico's Antiquated Secured Financing Law." *Arizona Journal of International and Comparative Law* 12, no. 523 (1995).

Meagher, Patrick. "Secured Finance for SMEs in Bangladesh." IRIS Center at the University of Maryland, College Park, 1998. http://www.iris.umd.edu/Reader.aspx?TYPE=FORMAL_PUBLICATION&ID=b08cf7d8-8bff-4221-979b-06c926321dc0.

Meyer, Richard L. "Performance of Rural Financial Markets: Comparative Observations from Asia, Latin America and the U.S." Paper presented at the annual meeting of the Brazilian Agricultural Economics Association (SOBER), Passo Fundo, Brazil, July 28–31, 2002. Ohio State University, Department of Agricultural, Environmental, and Development Economics, Rural Finance Program, Columbus. http://aede.osu.edu/programs/RuralFinance/Publications2002.htm.

Schreiner, Mark. "Microfinance in Rural Argentina." Microfinance Risk Management, Saint Louis, Mo.; and Washington University, Center for Social Development, Saint Louis, Mo., 2001. http://www.microfinance.com/English/Papers/Argentina_Rural_Microfinance.pdf.

Westley, Glenn D. "Can Financial Market Policies Reduce Income Inequality?" Sustainable Development Department Best Practices Series, MSM-112. Inter-American Development Bank, Washington, D.C., 2001.

Yaron, Jacob, McDonald Benjamin, and Stephanie Charitonenko. "Promoting Efficient Rural Financial Intermediation." *World Bank Research Observer* 13, no. 2 (1998): 147–70.

Yaron, Jacob, McDonald Benjamin, and Gerda L. Piprek. "The Legal and Regulatory Framework for Rural Financial Markets." In *Rural Finance: Issues, Design, and Best Practices.* Environmentally and Socially Sustainable Development Studies and Monographs Series, no. 14. Washington, D.C.: World Bank, 1997.

NOTES

1. See World Bank, "Principles and Guidelines on Effective Insolvency and Creditor Rights Systems" (Washington, D.C., 2001; http://web.worldbank.org/WBSITE/ EXTERNAL/TOPICS/LAWANDJUSTICE/GILD0,,language:120701~menuPK:14 6208~pagePK:181008~piPK:159223~theSitePK:215006,00.html), pp. 18–23; and UNCITRAL, *Report of Working Group VI (Security Interests) on the Work of Its Eighth Session (Vienna, 5–9 September 2005)*, A/CN.9/588 (2005; http://www. uncitral.org/uncitral/en/commission/working_groups/6Security_Interests.html).

2. For the EBRD model law, see John Simpson and Jan-Hendrik Röver, *Model Law on Secured Transactions* (London: EBRD, 2004; http://www.ebrd.com/pubs/ legal/5960.htm) (originally issued April 1993). For the OAS model law, see http:// www.oas.org/main/main.asp?sLang=E&sLink=http://www.oas.org/dil/.

3. Article 9 is available officially at http://www.law.upenn.edu/bll/ulc/ulc.htm#ucc9 but more conveniently at http://www.law.cornell.edu/ucc/ucc.table.html.

4. The convention is available at http://www.unidroit.org/english/conventions/ mobile-equipment/main.htm.

5. The convention is available at http://www.uncitral.org/uncitral/en/uncitral_ texts/payments/2001Convention_receivables.html.

6. For a general review of UNCITRAL's efforts in secured lending, see S. V. Bazinas, "UNCITRAL's Work in the Field of Secured Transactions," in Joseph J. Norton and Mads Andenas, eds., *Emerging Financial Markets and Secured Transactions* (The Hague: Kluwer Law International, 1998).

7. For a discussion of early experience with the EBRD model law, see Jan-Hendrik Röver, "An Approach to Legal Reform in Central and Eastern Europe: The European

Bank's Model Law on Secured Transactions," *European Journal of Law Reform* 1 (1998/99): 119–35. For more recent assessments, see the papers by Frédérique Dahan and by John Simpson posted on the EBRD website at http://www.ebrd. com/country/sector/law/st/new/index.htm.

8. See also publications listed at http://www.ebrd.com/country/sector/law/st/index. htm.

9. See discussion in Boris Kozolchyk and John M. Wilson, "The Organization of American States: The New Model Inter-American Law on Secured Transactions," *Uniform Law Review/Revue de droit uniforme* 7 (2002): 69–131.

10. See John Simpson and Jan-Hendrik Röver, *Model Law on Secured Transactions* (London: EBRD, 2004), p. 1; and Permanent Council of the OAS, Committee on Juridical and Political Affairs, "Inter-American Specialized Conferences on Private International Law: Report and Conclusions," OEA/Ser.G, CP/CAJP-2056/03 (2003; http://scm.oas.org/doc_public/ENGLISH/HIST_03/CP11200E04.doc#_Toc3808 4537), p. 5.

11. Available at http://www.med.govt.nz/media/20020501.html.

12. For examples of data from registries providing useful information about the registries' operation, including types of collateral taken, types of lenders and borrowers, and geographic location of filers, see Rodrigo Chaves, Nuria de la Peña, and Heywood Fleisig, "Secured Transactions Reform: Early Results from Romania," CEAL Issues Brief (Center for the Economic Analysis of Law, Washington, D.C., 2004). For an annotated version of the law, see Nuria de la Peña and Heywood Fleisig, "Romania: Law on Security Interests in Personal Property and Commentaries," *Review of Central and East European Law* 29, no. 2 (2004): 133–217.